# YANKELI
### (Yankee and Bengali)

## 10 Short Stories

# DILIP KUMAR MUKHERJEE

PHŒBE
MEDIA & PUBLISHING

Phoebe Media & Publishing and design are registered
trademarks of Phoebe Media & Publishing, Inc., the
publisher of this book. For information about special discounts
for bulk purchases, please contact Phoebe Media & Publishing at
customersupport@phoebepublishing.com. Phoebe Media & Publishing
can connect authors to your live event. For more information, contact
Phoebe Media & Publishing at customersupport@phoebepublishing.com
or visit our website at www.phoebepublishing.com.

Cover picture by Nisa Kuzukan
Cover and Interior design by April Basubas
Edited by Ann Downs
Library of Congress Cataloging-in-Publication Data is available

ISBN 978-1-7324987-6-1
LCCN:2020941177

*To my dearest, elder son, Jaydeep Mukherjee,*
*and*
*My dearest, younger son, Monideep Mukherjee,*
*With deep love and high regards.*
*'Baba'*

*Dilip Kr. Mukherjee*

# Author's Notes

The name of this story book is unusual. "Yankeli" is the cross-breed name for the American Yankee and Bengali cultures of a typical Bengali. In short, the mixing of words Yankee and Bengali makes it "Yankeli".

While working in the various states of America, the author had the opportunity of meditating with a variety of people. Particularly, the author noted that mixing with the American mainstream, his fundamental Indian values clashed with their ideas in every stage.

Sometimes, the age-old bonding had some funny outcomes. In this context, the differences within the first generation are more predominant than the second generation. In the time frame of sharing interior values, many cultural happenings may siphon off slowly.

Recently written, a few short stories published in newspapers and magazines in Calcutta have been added to this book. It is felt that the gracious feelings of all the countries are similar. Hence, the emotional "Yankeli" prosperity will be very beneficial.

Most of the stories consist of love affairs. They are based on different angles and with a variety of mentality. It is also presumed that life paths of different categories are interconnected. Other stories are based on various aspects of human life.

Good wishes,
Dilip Kr. Mukherjee
Austin, 2020

# Contents

# 1

## Pappoo and Santa Claus

The decision of Rameswar Misra's coming to America was not a correct one at all. He thought some problems would arise daily with his little son, Pappoo. Whether the problem was from him or his son, he didn't know clearly.

His wife, Sabitri, was a smart Indian housewife. She kept everything according to her husband's wishes. Rameswar was a curt, straight man; he didn't understand the world's phenomenon but understood the engineering process thoroughly. He had thus left everything in Sabitri's control, and he was kept away with office work. But in mind, when there is dirt in it, it cannot be easily removed. He did not want to look any further.

By chance, when Ram came to America and settled near Philadelphia, he never bothered with anything except his daily Hindu activities. Sabitri had no other alternative than to watch TV or read newspapers and magazines. Every day, she was discovering herself in the new environment. However, Pappoo was facing new kinds of difficulties. He couldn't speak the English language fluently. So, he couldn't mix with other children, but he keenly followed what other people were doing.

One day after school, Pappoo came home and tried to explain to his mom how, in the school lunch, he had enjoyed hamburger and beef patties. He liked them very much! Sabitri was afraid and asked him not to mention the beef patties to his father at all. Pappoo was curious about why the information should be painful to his father. However, Sabitri could not explain to Pappoo why his father's feelings would be hurt if he told him about the school lunches.

After a while, she said, "Look, we belong to the Hindu religion, and beef-eating is not allowed."

Pappoo still did not understand. Sabitri was annoyed at Pappoo's argument that his other Hindu friends ate beef patties with relish. "Is that not a violation of Hinduism, too?" Sabitri asked, in an intense voice. "Let's put that thing out of your mind, and nobody should listen to it."

Pappoo did not understand why things that were discussed in school could not fully be explained to his mother and not at all to his father. He felt something terrible in his heart; he felt very upset, but he couldn't explain what made him angry.

If in this hour, his own thick grandfather was with them, then the problem would never have existed. He thought about when his old grandfather would come to America, bringing lots of presents - including lots of sweets and candies. He missed very much his grandfather's "Ho-Ho-Ho" laughter!

Pappoo did not have many friends in the town. However, three blocks away, there lived a Jewish family with a Jewish boy of Pappoo's age, but he was not allowed to mix with any other local boys.

Pappoo stayed with his mom as much as he could. Eventually, Ram's family and the Jewish family become very close, mainly because of the friendship between the two boys. Pappoo even got permission to sleepover at the Jewish boy's house. Ram still liked the conservative way, to sleep and eat together in Indian style.

Life does not wait for anybody. Days passed by quickly, and Christmas came soon, too. Pappoo's little town suddenly burst with many lights and Christmas decorations. In almost every house, there were many Christ emblems with different statues. In every home, Pappoo saw different kinds of Christmas trees, very fancy and decorated with lots of typical Christmas decorations - with golden bulbs of various colors, many small hats, and numerous Christian playthings. Pappoo bargained with his mom to buy a Christmas tree that he could decorate like the rest of their neighbor's and his school friends.

At first, Sabitri did not notice when Pappoo kept insisting on getting a Christmas tree. Pappoo cried constantly about this, so Sabitri went to Ram to plead with him to buy a Christmas tree with decorations.

Ram flatly said, "No, we are not Christians. So, we do not need to purchase Christmas decorations for Christmas."

He had come to America directly from rural India, so he was not accustomed to the Christmas celebrations in America. While Pappoo was begging and pleading with him again and again, his father lost his control and sent him to his room. Pappoo went out, crying loudly. He then kept quiet for a day or two without talking to his father in order to show his anger.

Sabitri tried again, very quietly at first, to convince Ram to buy a Christmas tree.

Ram flatly replied, "A no answer is a flat no answer. In our house, there will not be any Christian celebration."

Sabitri appealed to Ram to buy a Christmas tree and asked, "What is the harm if somebody decorates a Christmas tree in one's house? You have not allowed Pappoo to celebrate for the Halloween festival; there are no puja celebrations like that in India. There is no kind of festival which Pappoo can enjoy. What is the harm to have a Christmas tree for Pappoo?"

But Ram said no to Sabitri - once and for all.

After that, there were several hours and no communication between them. When in bed, Sabitri again raised the question. Pappoo was crying loudly and that crying haunted her mind so very much.

3

She could not understand Ram's silly behavior, "Life is just like that - bizarre; after all, we have come to an unknown country. How long will you keep him under your protection? He is a young child, so why would he understand your strong medicine of religion?"

"Yet today, he will leave the social ups and downs, and tomorrow, he will leave the Hindu religion. After all, he will become an American-Sahib and will try to make us leave him alone," he continued. "Like other Americans, he will start to say, 'Leave me alone! It's my life!' I am just trying to halt that."

Sabitri persisted, "Will Pappoo remain under your skirt throughout his whole life? Look at you, could you stay in your Indian village forever?"

"Yes! True! I have come outside my house, but I have not changed my life. If everybody changes their life now, will the whole society stand still?"

"What happens to the damn bloody society, if there remains no pleasure in it?" Sabitri shouted.

"Today you are talking like an innocent child. If everyone breaks the rules, then what will happen to humanity? Have you observed the whole status of American society these days?"

After the quarrel, there was only silence between them. Sabitri was not convinced of Ram's logic. If this silly dirt covers your mind, plates will not be clean by washing alone.

From then on, life was pale and monotonous and full of grief for Pappoo. He did not talk to his father for a whole week despite the repeated coaxing from Ram.

Then, after a week, he started looking a little more joyful. He was again laughing, crying, and playing like before. Every time he played with Joseph, the Jewish boy, there were hushed talks and a little bit of a sly smile. In Joseph's house, there were no celebrations either, as they belonged to a strict Jewish family. Their home was quiet and similar to Pappoo's house.

In the meantime, Ram was teased by his office staff to go to their Christmas party. The day before Christmas, he decided to quietly write letters to his Indian relatives, but he couldn't avoid the friendly invitation from his colleagues. His colleagues wanted to introduce Ram to other Indian members of the same community. His house was not far away from theirs; about forty miles distant or over an hour journey.

After resisting many times, he agreed to visit his colleague's house on Christmas Eve. He thought he would take Pappoo along, too, to spend some time outside of the house. That would be good for his mental happiness. However, Pappoo did not want to go with them; he wanted to stay home. He would play with Joseph, whom he had invited for a sleepover. Eventually, Ram consulted Joseph's father, who said that he would come to the house and stay as a babysitter until 10 o'clock.

Ram's colleague's house was only forty miles away; if he left the party by 9:30, he could return to their house by 10:30 - just half an hour late. Joseph's father would watch TV, if by chance Ram and Sabitri were late; Joseph's father would lock Ram's front and back doors of the house, with the house key kept in a hidden place. So, Ram and Sabitri went to their friend's house without any worries.

Leaving Pappoo in the house by himself was not something Ram and Sabitri liked doing. Ram tried to think of a way he could soften Pappoo's heart. He believed the way he could do that was to come back early from his friend's house saying that he had to look after their child.

Ram went to the Christmas party, not knowing there were storm clouds in the sky. He thought that the celebration would only be for two hours, but when he reached his friend's house, he found a large crowd. There were all kinds of hot drinks, a big Christmas tree in the corner - beautifully decorated with small colored hats and gift boxes from Santa Claus.

Santa Claus's gifts were distributed among the children after dinner, as they were playing merrily in the next room. Everybody in that room was dressed for Christmas celebrations, with Christmas hats and other beautiful things.

After seeing the noisy atmosphere, Sabitri began enjoying the festivities and wondering how she could include Pappoo in the party, too. She told the housewife her thoughts; she had not understood that this was going to be a Christmas party. The lady, after hearing Sabitri's story, told her to take an extra pack of pastries with a gift box for Pappoo. Sabitri was very happy after hearing this.

With the arrival of more and more guests, the party became very hilarious and noisy. Ram was feeling restless, and after about an hour, he realized snow had been falling continuously the entire time they had been at the party. The snow was filling up the highways.

Around 9 o'clock, he could not remain idle any longer; at last, around 10 o'clock, he decided to leave the party. Ram wished his colleagues a Merry Christmas, promising to bring Pappoo next time. He and Sabitri went to their car when a strong wind suddenly swept through the open door. Another friend shouted in a loud, jolly voice, "It will be a white Christmas...a most beautiful Christmas!"

Ram thought that the distance home was only 40 miles; if he could drive quickly, he would reach his house in approximately one hour. In the meantime, about 1 1/2 feet of snow had accumulated on the road. The car began to skid, and the visibility was poor. Ram was unaccustomed to driving in snow, so it took nearly 2 1/2 hours to travel only 40 miles; it was 12 midnight when they arrived at home.

Hesitantly, he parked the car in the garage; he and Sabitri entered the sitting room quickly. Joseph's father had left around 11 o'clock, leaving a note on the table. The paper read, "Everything is okay here- goodnight - shalom." Both husband and wife thought that Pappoo and his friend must be sleeping in Pappoo's bedroom. Entering the kitchen, Sabitri turned on the light, drank a glass of water, and left the gift packets on the table. She placed the pastry boxes inside the fridge and started talking to Ram in a twisted tongue.

"Oh yes! You may be a conservative man, but without any hesitation, you drank three pegs of whiskey - one after another! Is that not a correct fact?"

Ram answered absentmindedly, "The guests were looking at me. To save my prestige, I had to drink three whiskey pegs. To keep the mind healthy, with a little bit of twisting the pride, that is not harmful!"

"Oh yes! Come now! To break the rule is not a crime, but if the rule is broken by little Pappoo, that becomes a criminal thing, isn't it?"

"Who wants to do a random thing in front of a new crowd?" he asked. "Nothing happens if you bend the rules a bit?"

"Then why did you not buy the little child the Christmas tree he wanted for a mere ten dollars?"

"Look - ten dollars is not a lot of money; it is very little. The real story is the Indian principle of no Christian celebrations."

"Oh God! Indians came to America to earn money by any means. You want to save the money that way, isn't it?" Sabitri snapped.

"Are you now saying that the Indian principle is terrible?"

"It is not bad, but it could be worse. Whenever trouble comes, Indians start merrily flying kites in the sky, right?"

Ram wanted to argue a bit, but he found little truth in what Sabitri said. Before any further talk, he said calmly, "Let's go to sleep. It is getting late."

The husband and wife slowly went upstairs without creating any sound to disturb the sleeping children. She opened Pappoo's room door very slowly and looked inside, but she couldn't find Pappoo or Joseph at all.

She shouted at the top of her voice, "The kids are not here in the room."

Ram cried from the next room, "Well, the kids might have slept in the guest room."

Both Ram and Sabitri ran to the guest room but found no one there. Both husband and wife became worried. Where had the children gone? Did they go to Joseph's house to sleep? That was not possible. Outside there was snow, and besides, both front and back doors were locked. They came back to their sitting room to find the room empty.

Sabitri almost fainted from fear; she just kept saying, "Oh God! What has happened? Let us call the police!"

Ram, too, became afraid, but said gently, "Let us think together slowly about where the kids could be."

Suddenly, both remembered to look in the basement! Running breathlessly, they opened the basement door, and the basement light was on. On the floor, the two kids were sleeping in their own sleeping bags, side by side. Their faces were soft and peaceful. Faint smiles warmed their faces as if they had drowned themselves in sweet dreams.

In the corner, there was a foot-tall Christmas tree. The red and blue icicles were hanging from the tree at various angles. Ram and Sabitri had not seen the tree earlier. Where had the small Christmas tree come from? Convenient stores were close to their house. They must have collected one of them and hid in it the basement. The tree had stockings from Santa Claus; there were also small gift packages lying peacefully underneath the tree. On each package, haphazardly written in uneven letters, was the children's handwriting. Two parcels had two words, one from Pappoo and the other from Joseph. On the other closed packages were the names of Ram, Sabitri, and Joseph's parents; the last two packages contained the name of Pappoo's granddad and Joseph's dog. While the children were arranging the gifts, they had fallen asleep and decided to sleep in the basement.

Pappoo's father is a conservative Hindu; he did not want any Christmas decorations in his house. Joseph's father was a basic Jewish man, so he did not want any Christmas celebration either. But who can stop the bulky Santa Claus from moving from house to house? Santa was neither Hindu nor Jewish; he was simply an aged, fat, old man with a bag of gifts on his shoulder who laughs abruptly, "Ho-ho-ho-ho!" He does not ask what to read and how to write but goes on saying funny stories.

For a long time, Ram and Sabitri watched them quietly. Then, Ram suggested they let them sleep peacefully, while in the morning, they could take them upstairs to their beds.

They left the basement door slightly open; the bright, shining light coming from the star at the top of the tree. Ram's mind shivered like a wink. The shadow from the Christmas tree was like a church shadow. The two boys looked like pilgrims who were waiting at the church door but had fallen asleep. Slowly and steadily, Ram's mind opened its doors. As if from the basement, an open road had spread itself toward infinity. There will be so many pilgrims who will come through that road - one by one.

Pappoo was dreaming of Santa Claus. He knew Santa would come soon with his bag; his carriage would be running at high speed on top of the ice. If the old grandpa came out on the roadway, it would be wonderful! It was likely his grandpa had understood Pappoo's Christmas wishes, and he had taken his horse-drawn carriage and gone to locate Pappoo's house. All around him, there was a flurry of snowflakes. Grandpa felt very cold, so he covered himself with a red coat and a red winter hat. Surprisingly, the horse-drawn carriage slowly turned into a sleigh drawn by reindeer. The sleigh held several bags containing flutes, picture books, and lots of sweetmeats. There were laddoo and peras; there were jilebi, the sweet, puffed biscuits. Everything Pappoo loved was there! As soon as the reindeer smelled the sweat meats, they started running faster and faster.

The fat, old grandpa shouted, "Do not run too fast! Be careful! Be careful! Ho-ho-ho-ho!"

At that moment, the bells around the necks of the reindeer started ringing simultaneously - Jingle bell! Jingle bell! Jingle bell! The constant ringing of the bells sounded like his grandpa's old horse carriage! He knew his grandpa was coming today to his house...and he was dressed just like Santa Claus! He would arrive soon...Ho! Ho! Ho! Ho!

# 2

## Second Love

Early in the morning, the Calcutta Express left Siliguri station. Coming from the nearby town of Darjeeling Garden, Namita came with her son to wish her husband, Tapan, bon voyage. Tapan worked in a tea garden as an accountant cum clerk. The tea garden was almost three miles from Darjeeling; Tapan had to go to Calcutta for a financial briefing. Darjeeling Proper is cold and full of snowfall during the winter months, but Tapan had to stay in the cold because of the Workforce Code of Conduct. His salary was nominal, so his wife had to accept a low post as a school teacher.

The sun rising in the sky was barely visible. The whole atmosphere was dark and covered by clouds. The cold air was blowing angrily across the platform. The taxi drivers were clothed in heavy winter clothes, waiting for the occasional rider. In the winter season, the afternoon train had few passengers. The number of rides for Darjeeling and Kalimpong were much less during that time of year.

In the empty railway station, Mr. Sarkar was waiting in his heavy suit with his thick over-coat on top. The cold wind was pushing and shoving the ordinary riders, but Mr. Sarkar was calmly walking on the platform as if the wind had no effect on him. In fact, the icy wintertime made him feel quite peaceful.

The drivers of the vans were searching here and there for prospective passengers. One driver from Nepal gave a smart salute in front of Mr. Sarkar and said in a very solemn voice, "Sir, my van is very comfortable; it drives with speed."

Mr. Sarkar did not answer and continued walking. The van, whether empty or full, was no bother to him. Van riders were roaming everywhere, he knew that, so he was not concerned about being without a ride.

The waiting room door opened suddenly; Mr. Sarkar saw a long overcoat wrapped over a bright sari - a young lady coming out of the waiting room. With a small finger gripped tightly in her hand, he saw the lady walking with a little, two-year-old boy. His first thought - she was enchanting like a floating, drifting firefly! The vision flooded Mr. Sarkar's imagination. She was walking to a seat, and the young child, like a second sweet fruit, was hanging at her side.

The girl's skin was a delicious brown-color; her figure was slim and agile, and she had large brown eyes. The boy was an energetic toddler with a blunt nose and small, inquisitive eyes. Sarkar was looking at them through his glasses. He decided not to stay there, standing in the cold, any longer.

He watched a Nepali driver whisper something to the girl; something in a hidden manner. Sarkar was a businessman, so he understood that the woman was trying to negotiate a cheaper ride. He immediately called the Nepali driver with the intention of hiring him. The driver saluted Sarkar for the second time – with a little more politeness in his voice than before.

Sarkar asked him, "What is the condition of the van? Will it run the whole distance to Darjeeling?"

The Nepali driver answered with an assuring voice, "Yes sir! The van is in excellent condition! An American car."

"Ok, let's go."

"It would be better if you allow me to carry other passengers, too," the driver said.

"Alright, if you wish to earn a little extra money, you can take on another fair. But look here, not more than one extra passenger." Sarkar was thinking how nice it would be if the girl accompanied him. Usually, in a normal situation, he would travel alone without any other passengers at all. Three big suitcases, one big hold-all, and a few leather bags that were Sarkar's luggage – all were piled into the van. While the driver could easily carry another person, he was delighted to know that he had come to some sort of bargain fare with the girl. Sarkar observed all these things quietly.

The girl had very little luggage - one ordinary suitcase, a thin bedspread, and a pillow. The girl and child advanced to the van. Sarkar, with no more room in the back seat, sat next to the driver in the front. The driver operated the van at a high rate of speed, especially considering the winter weather. In the back seat, a family was sitting, which brought him some kind of satisfaction. That is why, even if he paid the full fare to the driver, he did not feel he was doing anything wrong. No indiscretions.

While seeing ditches and driving on winding roads, the child began to jump up and down in the van with excitement. The girl was uncomfortable with the child's bold actions. As he jumped, the small boy touched the dress of Sarkar. Though the girl was embarrassed by this, both Sarkar and the boy started laughing. The boy then crawled into the front seat. The child's soft touch on Sarkar's fatherly instincts was a soothing touch; this gave Sarkar a sudden feeling as if something were missing in his life.

Sarkar had always analyzed his lifestyle slightly like a film. His mother had died much earlier, and after his father died, he was forced to quit his studies. Finding no other way to maintain his livelihood and as everything flashed before his eyes, he took the job of a contract worker for a meager wage. Finally, he started a contract business for constructing houses.

Once he had been going from house to house, begging for money, but today he could handle tons and tons of cash with no problem. That is why Sarkar understood the value of money so emphatically.

While earning wealth, he was getting older day by day, but with the greed for money, he could not focus on anything else. But, other than money, what else had he earned? Now, neither of his parents were alive, and he did not have any brothers or sisters. So, he just focused on earning money and thought that money would take care of everything.

He had also earned his reputation in life. He had befriended people, both socially and politically, but what was the actual benefit? He still felt no one really knew who he was, and sometimes, like today, he felt lonely as well.

There were plenty of insincere love and phony friendships for Sarkar, but those games were played in hopes of catching him unawares. So now he avoided those people altogether; nothing attracted him now. Lots of bees hummed around his pot of honey, but he shunned them entirely. So, he was earning money as if it were an addiction; no other work attracted him more than the money-making business.

During the rainy season, the small ponds of the road canal would sweep into his money flow; the money came to his pocket relentlessly. However, he did not care for it anymore. He no longer worried about his personal habits; he did not care for mundane routines. He remained alone. So, how would he spend this massive amount of money? His personal expenses were only five thousand dollars. His only expensive habit was to eat in fine restaurants and to eat different kinds of food.

But today, playing with the boy in the cold weather, was soothing him very much. The boy settled into Sarkar's lap and was giggling in a lively way as he watched the world go by. To Sarkar, the experience was very peculiar. A silent feeling of love was flowing through his body.

The flower blossoms on the tree started loving the tree itself. It was as if she were that kind of woman who keeps a loving watch over her child and maintains the fire of any man's wishes. In her quiet laugh, there were splashes of lively youth, but inside her heart, the touch of love was there. Such a natural feeling, Sarkar's body timidly felt these emotions.

The van was climbing gradually on the snake-like, bending road. With the cold weather came drops of rain; the wipers were clearing the rain from the windshield. From inside, the toddler was trying to touch the wiper as it went back and forth, back and forth. But he could not catch them - even though Sarkar was guiding the toddler's hands - because the wipers were outside the glass. For whatever reason, Sarkar did not want to release those tiny fingers.

The boy suddenly noticed Sarkar's tie pin, but before he could grab for it, Sarkar removed the tie pin from his coat and fixed it on the child's clothing. He also removed his grey colored sunglasses and fixed them over the toddler's eyes. The sunglasses covered half of his face, and the child kept laughing at that notion.

Sarkar noticed in the reflection of the glass that the boy's mother was trying desperately to keep the toddler quiet. Sarkar, after seeing that, turned his head towards her and told her not to worry - everything was ok. The lady smiled at those words.

In the meantime, the driver was slowly moving the vehicle through the rain and snow, and in a terrifying tone, told Sarkar that outside the rain was falling in torrents. "I do not know how far I can drive in this bad weather," the driver declared.

In reply, Sarkar told him to take the van to the nearest rest house. Water was flowing like a waterfall from both sides of the van; the car could only move a little at a time in the winter weather and dense fog.

After a while, the driver halted the van almost fifteen miles away from the Kalimpong area's rest house. They had come so near to Darjeeling, but they still couldn't reach it. The driver pulled the van into the parking lot of the rest house. There he saw a few local people with their cars and vans drenched in rainwater and under whatever shelter they could find. They were saying the rain might cause a landslide on the way to Darjeeling.

As the driver opened the door of the van, Sarkar emerged, clinging to the toddler's thumb. Namita, the boy's mother, came down next. The orderly saluted them and addressed the untimely guests; the butler asked about brunch in the morning and the noontime meal; did the guests want them prepared? Sarkar, without looking at the girl, gave yes as an answer. Namita had brought a milk bottle for her son, and he realized the affordability of brunch was not easy for her.

Namita called her son, "Biltu, will you come here to drink your milk?"

After they were served brunch by the butler, the orderly and the butler had assumed the three of them were a family. Namita was taken aback by this idea and said politely to Sarkar, "No, I do not eat now."

Sarkar quietly told her, in this cold weather, a cup of tea with a biscuit would be a welcome surprise.

Sarkar broke a piece of omelet and gave it to Biltu; the toddler pleasantly tested this new delight. Sarkar began laughing quietly and started giving him a piece of every morsel the butler served. Unexpectedly, the child, after receiving all adult foods, was eating everything with delight.

Namita looked at them and started to say, "Do not give him so much food; the child can't eat it all."

Sarkar smiled and tried to make conversation with Namita. He asked her, "Are you a resident in Darjeeling?"

Namita said hesitantly, "Yes, we live very near Darjeeling. I am Namita Chowdhuri, wife of Tapan Chowdhuri. We are returning to Darjeeling after sending off Mr. Chowdhuri to the Calcutta Express."

Sarkar continued, "What does Mr. Chowdhuri do in Darjeeling?"

Namita answered, "Mr. Chowdhuri is an accountant in a tea garden near Darjeeling, and I am a schoolteacher nearby. Are you travelling in Darjeeling?"

Sarkar smiled gently and said, "In this cold weather, is anybody going travelling? No, I am going for my business transaction, but I do admit that Darjeeling is a nice town, with pleasant weather and beautiful places."

Namita asked inquiringly, "You did not bring your wife because you came here for a business transaction?"

Sarkar answered hesitantly, "No, I do not have a wife. I am not married." Then, after halting a bit, Sarkar said, "You know that Darjeeling's new church is built by me? Now, many buildings in Darjeeling are constructed by me."

Resting his arms on the table, Sarkar closely observed Namita and her child. She had fine hair with a lovely figure; she was a good-looking woman. Sarkar was clearly looking at her body with his piercing eyes. She began to feel a warm feeling and asked hurriedly, "The rain is falling heavily. How will we reach Darjeeling on time?"

From his pocket, Sarkar took out a gold cigarette box and lit an aristocratic cigarette. He told her the rain might not stop at all, and the landslides may not be cleaned in time.

"If you don't reach Darjeeling on time, what will happen?" he asked.

Namita sounded a little worried when she told him she was to go to school tomorrow morning by any means. She then said, "You have come here for business; there may be a lot of financial loss for you if you do not make it there."

"Yes, the job to be done tomorrow may not be done, but it can be done the day after tomorrow."

He asked the butler to bring the bill. He told Namita that when he was young, the word "school" repelled him; now, her keenness to return to her school made him feel just the opposite.

"You no longer have an interest in your construction job?" she asked.

"I have never thought about that, but it is now that I think I am slowly driving my life's carriage through a muddy road."

In the meantime, the driver came back to the table and told them the road to Darjeeling was completely closed. Sarkar called the police station to double-check and got the same reply. They told him it would take ten to twelve hours to clear the road. That meant they had to stay in the rest house for the whole night.

He asked the orderly to bring the bed and other luggage inside. Because the orderlies thought that they were of the same family, they kept their beds side by side. He would construct the army barracks near the Jalaphar area of Darjeeling as early as possible. In the meantime, he would stay the night at Windamere hotel, which was the costliest in the whole of Darjeeling. Namita was amazed that he would be staying at such a fancy hotel.

She immediately said, "My husband is an accountant; in fact, he is a part-time clerk and earns a basic salary, pretty low."

Sarkar knew Namita worked at a school mistress's job, which also was a low salary. He knew the cost of the hotel was too much for her to pay.

Namita snatched her son before he could investigate Sarkar's watch and said, "You better keep your watch within your possession, or Biltu might break it."

Biltu was almost crying, and Namita urged him to stop; otherwise, his uncle would discipline him. The word "uncle" as her relation would indeed keep him under control.

After dinner, they were sitting in the lounge when Namita began to feel cold. Biltu was sleeping in bed, so Sarkar told her to go upstairs, too.

She asked, "And you, where will you be?"

"I do not feel sleepy. You know, I have a marriage proposal with my relative's daughter."

"So, why do you not marry her?" Namita asked.

"I have spent forty-six years of my life as a bachelor; I can spend the rest of my life as a bachelor, too. You know marriage is like a gamble. Let it remain as it is."

Sarkar told Namita to go inside and try to get some sleep. Shivering from the cold, Namita said, "Let's both go to bed. In our house, we sleep in the same room all the time due to shortage of space. In bed, everybody sleeps with his or her blanket covers."

Sarkar was thinking how lucky he was with one voluptuous girl sleeping close to him like his wife and the boy in between. It was a picture of an entire household affair, and he smiled at the thought.

The next morning, they started their journey to Darjeeling; the road had been cleaned during the night.

Sarkar said, "I do not feel happy to leave this rest house, do you know the reason?"

Namita shyly lowered her face and remained speechless. She understood her husband as timid and generally, a good gentleman. She loved him that way, the attraction between man and woman strictly adhered to it. He was her first love, but Sarkar seemed to be a different man. He was very open-minded, liberal in faith; his deep and quiet liking to her was too implicit. She couldn't open her mouth; a woman is always defeated by a man's talk in this respect whether the woman feels at peace or is in turmoil. But here, the feelings were one-sided – nothing more, nothing else.

Before continuing to Darjeeling, Sarkar said in a tentative voice, "If you have no objections, can I take a few photos of both you and Biltu? Let me keep it as a memento."

Namita wholeheartedly agreed with that proposal, and she looked to Sarkar. She stood there stylishly with her neck bent slightly like a cinema actress. Sarkar took his time taking his pictures.

Over the next six months, there was a tremendous change in both their lifestyles. Tapan Chowdhuri left his job as a tea garden accountant cum clerk position and became the chief accountant of Sarkar Brothers Company; his salary increased by eight times.

Namita was no more an ordinary school teacher. She stayed at home, and under the mild sunshine, she spent her time stitching blouses and woolen sweaters. A poor Nepali girl looked after Biltu while she strolled. The complete change of lifestyles was taking place gradually.

Sarkar had to come to Darjeeling often to observe the work of his construction in Jalaphar's Army barracks. He came to Namita's house often, and without saying many words, she would sit gracefully like a glorious statue in Sarkar's mind while he merely watched her every move. Sarkar gifted her colorful saris, jewelry, and other materials, which she had to wear in front of him. In fact, she liked to dress in Sarkar's style.

One day, Sarkar stayed in her house quite late, but he did not touch her; instead, he sat at a distance and gazed at her beauty.

He said, "Namita, I love you. I have no plan for a proposal, no motive behind it. You are the picture in my heart. I want to see you always and feel that you are mine alone."

Namita understood what Sarkar was trying to say; she moved slowly to the window and stood like a statue for a long time. She was thinking of how Sarkar gave so much, how he was a good person, and how he had changed her life. Namita so far had not given him anything in return.

Of course, Sarkar had lost himself in his imagination, but he had quickly done that with a wizard's sickening touch. That touch is known by a man like Sarkar only; there was no way she could escape from him. Not even her son, Biltu, or her husband, Tapan, knew the secret. As if they had sold their wishes to Sarkar's wizards.

Sarkar came back day after day; it was always the same thing he uttered in the very same way, "I want you, Namita."

She couldn't say no to him. Namita loved him from the core of her heart, but the love was generated by the heart he gave to her. She loved her husband for one reason, and she loved Sarkar for another reason. In India, to love two men at the same time was unheard of and illegal; one woman cannot have two husbands in any country.

So, what could she do? To say no to Sarkar? But she had no reason. Again, to get a divorce from her husband couldn't be done because she loved him as well.

Namita had lost her right to enjoy both men because she loved them from the deepest part of her heart. Sarkar eyed Namita with a yearning look in his eyes, but her love for him was in her mind and her heart. Sarkar's real love, bodily desire, could it surpass the love she felt? That is an affair of one's flesh to another's flesh and nothing else. Is that called real love? The man who desperately wanted her; that love was like forcefully plucking a flower in a garden. Is that real love? Does that not create a cry of torture?

Yes, Namita loved both men. She loved them with her mind and with her heart and did not want to lose either of them. What type of dilemma was Namita in?

To love both men together is probably the right answer. God knows, no gentleman would agree with Namita's mind. And no girl would agree with Namita either. But Namita is Namita; she did not want to be another type of girl but herself. Then, what shall she do now?

# 3

## New Generation

*Chapter One*

It was a warm afternoon in May and Kalyan was heading home from school with loads of papers under his arm. As he opened the door, the wind swung the door open and struck him with tremendous force. Sujata, his seven-months pregnant wife, could not suppress her laughter. She started laughing slowly at first; then, burst into fits of laughter. After Kalyan finished collecting his school papers from the ground, he said angrily, "My face has just been flattened by the door and you can't stop laughing..."

Before Kalyan could finish his sentence, Sujata started laughing again as if she couldn't stop herself. "Someone," she said, "is making me laugh! I cannot control myself!"

"Now, not only are you laughing with your whole body, but you are claiming someone else is forcing you to laugh. Are you going mad?"

"No, I am all right, but I have the feeling someone else is controlling me and making me do awkward things!"

"You were home alone all day and getting bored. That is why you are having a hard time controlling your laughter. The insanity has gone to your head!"

"I don't understand why I am doing these crazy things - I truly do not know. But if you are preparing tea for yourself, would you make some for me, too?"

Kalyan replied, "The doctor has told you to drink milk during your pregnancy because tea will create acidity in your body. That acidity will then create headaches for you, do you understand?"

"You must prepare tea for me now – no milk! Something is teasing me again and again and telling me to drink tea."

"So, you are forcing me to make tea? Show me that pregnancy book!"

Without talking, Sujata passed the book to Kalyan. The book showed a pregnant woman carrying an unborn child with his head facing downward. Kalyan told her the child would slide down when it was ready to be born and would start crying in a tough voice, "M-aa-a, M-aa-a."

Before Kalyan could finish his "m-aa-a call", from Sujata's mouth came a loud yell in a goat's voice..."Mah-mah-mah!"

Kalyan was surprised, "Why are you calling your mother? Your mother is not here."

"Yes, I know that," said Sujata, and before she could answer, she opened her mouth wide and released a huge yawn.

The ear-splitting noise of her yawn threw Kalyan back against the wall. He wondered why she had yawned so loudly.

After Kalyan prepared the tea, Sujata sat quietly and drank the entire cup. Before Kalyan knew it, she cried out again in a goat-like voice, "Mah! Mah!"

Sujata took Kalyan's hand and pleaded, "It wasn't me who cried like a goat! Believe me, I am telling the truth! I didn't want to yawn or speak with a goat's voice. Neither did I mean to laugh at you when you accidentally ran into the front door."

"Do you mean to tell me someone else is doing all these awkward things?"

"You may laugh at what I'm telling you, but I promise these are not my actions. They are the actions of our unborn child; he is the one who is doing these ghostly things!"

"Do you mean to say our unborn child, Khoka, is doing all these peculiar things?" Kalyan exclaimed.

"I was afraid you would not believe me. Here...see for yourself. Put your hands on my stomach and wait."

Then Sujata shouted into the air, "Khoka, my child. Please raise my stomach three times if you want to drink another cup of tea."

Kalyan was astonished as the baby kicked her stomach three times. He didn't understand this child – was it a boy or a girl – who was doing all this kicking?

Sujata, on the other hand, was calmly saying, "Khoka, my son, Khoka." She smiled and looked at Kalyan and told him Khoka was intentionally doing all these awkward things. She had not done anything.

Kalyan brought his wife a second cup of tea, and she drank it quietly, waiting for his reaction. When she was finished, she began yawning again; loud and ear-shattering noises filled the air. Kalyan was again thrown back against the wall by the unexpected sound. If this truly was the unborn child's idea of a joke, then it would be a boy and not a girl; a girl would not be this mischievous! Yes, his unborn son definitely had a compelling voice!

While sleeping at night, Sujata said, "Kalyan, did you know that I have read the pregnancy book for the second time? The book says sometimes cells in the unborn child's brain can grow abruptly – more than other parts of the body. If that is what's happening – if the baby's brain is gaining the capacity of an adult - how can we stop that?"

"Our son is not a toad; you are reading too many books these days. You are the one who is picking up peculiar habits, not our child, because of all the books you are reading!"

"No, I am not the one with this peculiar habit. It is Khoka who wants to read books on many subjects; he wants to learn many things quickly."

"What are you saying? A baby's brain cannot digest many things at the same time, especially when he has not even been born yet! Now, may I please go to sleep?"

Sujata knew within one day she hadn't been mistaken. Her mother's anxiety forced the unborn child to tell her that he was a boy and not a girl. Sujata, as well as Kalyan, was puzzled and surprised that the unborn child didn't like hard meat; he didn't like old music, and he wanted to read difficult books. Kalyan eventually accepted Khoka's wild behavior. Kalyan said, "I think I will give him a separate name."

"You are the person who should name the child – you are the schoolteacher!"

"We will keep the name 'Nobu', or a new one, that will be fitting for this boy."

"When he grows older, the alternate name will be added to his surname. The thing you must remember is Nobu should not yawn so viciously in front of others! Let him show the world how powerful his brain is; the whole world will be astonished! To be an ordinary schoolteacher's father should not be anybody's wistfulness."

### Chapter Two

On Friday, Kalyan took Sujata to Dr. Goswami's office. The office looked exceptionally clean and in tiptop shape. The back wall of his office consisted of the doctor's professional certificates. The rest of the walls contained only the pictures of little toddlers...all looking like smiling, growing flowers. Dr. Goswami asked Sujata how she was feeling.

"I am alright, but from time to time, I can't keep from yawning. In my leisure time, I tend to read lots of books - unnecessary books

– ones in which I have no interest! I also feel like eating different kinds of food which I have never liked. My husband thinks I am going mad!"

"No, no, no," the doctor said with a smiling face. "This is a natural phenomenon; your pregnancy has made you change your taste in food and has created a bilious eructation. Forgive me for using medical vocabulary...do you feel any pinching?"

"Yes, the unborn child is creating plenty of pinching with his legs."

"Headaches, vomiting tendency, or swelling of legs and hands are all normal. Is there anything severely irregular?" the doctor continued.

"No, nothing is irregular."

"You are in excellent condition; let me examine the child once more. Slowly lay down on that table."

The doctor called the nurse to help her lie down. Then, he used his stethoscope and started to slowly push her belly in many spots. Suddenly, his eyebrows began to twitch. His moustache stood erect like scorpion stings...they seemed to start dancing!

Sujata was surprised to see a change in the doctor's face and said, "Doctor, is there something wrong with the child?"

The doctor somehow managed to control his dancing moustache with his left hand; he groaned quietly and said, "Either somebody is experimenting with a ham-radio with foul language, or maybe something is wrong with my stethoscope. Let me change it quickly."

Dr. Goswami left the room and returned with a new stethoscope, eager to continue the examination. This time, when he started examining Sujata's stomach, the result was the same. The doctor's face became greenish-yellow; his ears were full of a whistling sound. He put the stethoscope to Sujata's ear.

With his stethoscope, she could hear her unborn son's voice very clearly. The voice was distinctly saying, "The doctor is a nuisance with a bad cigarette smell on his fingers; he just examined me by pressing me and making me move up and down. Please supply him a few bottles of laxatives so that he will lie on the bed for a whole day without doing anything."

Sujata was very embarrassed; then, she realized the doctor had vanished into his office, which was adjacent to the veranda, and started nervously smoking a cigarette. His hands were moving everywhere like the wings of an airplane, and his legs were shaking like steel springs. After some time, a nurse entered the examining room and told Sujata she could go home because the exam was over. She then told her when to return for her final examination before the delivery.

Back at home, when Kalyan heard the details, his heart almost collapsed. He shouted at Sujata, "What if our son turns out to be a genius? What if he turns out to be a foul-language boy?"

"Do not shout so loudly! Our unborn son, Nobu, does not like shouting. If you continue, he will start kicking my stomach repeatedly."

After a while, he thought there might be a connection between his son's discussions about bed pans and his use of purgatives – even though they were both bad topics.

"I also do not know how he communicates with me. Perhaps through my nerves? Through a telepathic message?"

"If it happens through the nerves, that is hard to understand. How are you singing all the hymns in Sanskrit and Hindi? How do you know what to say? Hindi and Sanskrit are not your mother's language."

"Nobu, the unborn child, is a genius; he can learn and speak any language very quickly. He just flips through the pages of the books, and when he is finished, he knows things perfectly - just like a professor. So, now he has mastered physics, chemistry, biology, along with details of literature and poems. Nobu has exceeded even you in knowledge, Kalyan. If he reads any more books, he will finish and get a PhD degree in no time!"

Kalyan did not like Nobu's uncontrolled knowledge, but he had one more question to ask Sujata. Forgetting his inquisitiveness, he asked, "I realize that Nobu can understand you, and you can understand him pretty well. But how can Nobu understand other people's minds? How does he learn so quickly?"

"He understands the thoughts of others equally as well. The other day, he clearly told me your English accent is pretty awful. You used the word "vice-chancellor", but you did not have the correct pronunciation. You said, 'wich canchelor' and 'mayher desk' in place of – 'megher desh.'"

Hearing his son's advice, Kalyan became outraged, and he started expressing his anger. Sujata cut him off and said, "You cannot sleep beside me if you are going to act that way."

Kalyan's mouth dropped open in astonishment, "Then where should I sleep? Should I sleep with somebody else's wife?"

"No, I did not say that. Nobu, our child, tells me that he is getting older, so it is not a good thing for you to be flippant with him."

"Nobu is not only getting older, but he has turned into a monkey!"

Kalyan gave up, took his pillow, and went to the next room to sleep alone.

Sujata was now eight months pregnant, and Nobu was quickly learning astrophysics, architecture, law, business management, medicine, and modern literature through his variety of books. In fact, he did not like ordinary books any longer. Sujata quickly turned the pages of any book Nobu wanted to read, and the child learned the subject immediately. Sujata sometimes called him a monkey, or hyena, or kangaroo, but she was confident that after the delivery, her son would be world-famous!

Nobu tried to add variety to his diet; for the first time, he tried bread fried with kin seed oil. The next three days, he tried eating fish with jam. He also tried vegetables and salted potatoes. Showing no sign of giving in, Sujata followed her son's instructions regarding eating.

She knew that, eventually, their picture would be in the newspaper and movies would be made of their lives. Both Kalyan and she would earn loads of money because of their genius son.

Suddenly, Nobu insisted she should start writing for him. He began dictating to Sujata his thoughts - the famous piece of classical literature, Gita, was incomplete. So, he began writing an addition to Gita with more clarification on *The Sacred Song of God*:

"In the cold wintery night, tough people smoke Indian hemp.

In festival time, you can use a pungent drink,

But tea drinking happens every night.

Sometimes, you eat tamarind but never romantic cocaine.

In an empty stomach, never take aromatic acridity."

A wise teacher could not write a poem of this nature, but on the other hand, this unborn child, while studying quantum mechanics, had written a full-fledged, Sanskrit poem.

Next, Nobu wrote a parody of Tagore's poem, *The Dirty Pond has a Broken Dream.*

"I will break even my dusty hair.

I will smash my body with dirty soil.

I will use a throwaway loin cloth on top of my body."

"Why is the fourth line vacant?" Kalyan asked.

Sujata replied, "The boy said the fourth line is too dirty to write in words."

Kalyan attentively listened to these hymns, but as soon as he listened to the dirty wording, he became furious. He was afraid Nobu would become a dirty rogue!

Sujata said, "When Nobu gets older, the wrong, useless words will be lost to him."

"What does Nobu want to do when he gets older?" Kalyan wondered.

"He hasn't indicated that yet, but tomorrow, he told me he will try to write a novel. The name of the book will be *Callous Cordiality*, and it will be a significant piece of literature. The subject matter will include love, fighting, self-esteem, and satanic performance."

By the end of the next five days, Nobu had not finished one-third of the novel. Even though neither Kalyan nor Sujata knew much about publishing a book, Kalyan signed his name at the bottom of the partially finished novelette anyway.

It was strange that the future publisher of the book wrote a letter to Kalyan stating the partly written novelette was of excellent quality; he asked Kalyan to sign a contract before the final publication. In the meantime, he sent Kalyan a cheque of two hundred dollars as an advance on the contract.

For two days, the house cleaners did not come to their home, so Kalyan had to do all the house chores himself. He did the work because he did not want to bother Sujata; he wanted her and Nobu to finish writing *Callous Cordiality*.

Kalyan shouted from a distance, "Sujata, how far is Nobu with finishing the novel?"

"Nobu has not finished writing the novel. The main characters, Ram and Shyam, are two kinds of computer software. They started loving the keyboard of the lady computer, Linda. But Linda does not like Ram and Shyam; she likes a different computer hardware, Robert. However, Robert's hardware does not love Linda back; he loves Jenny's language. Jenny does not love any of Ram, Shyam, or Robert's computer parts. Instead, Jenny loves John's processor, but John, again, does not love..."

"What is the matter with Nobu? It looks like love is becoming a recurring theme in this novel; A does not love B and B does not love C. How many heroes and heroines are in the novel?"

"Well, Nobu says that all computer languages change every year, so that is the reason Nobu chose the novel's title – *Callous Cordiality* – because it means the computers' love is very callous."

Kalyan went back to the kitchen to prepare boiled lady's finger for Nobu. After starting the novel, Nobu had started eating okra four times a day. Sujata never liked okra because they float buoyantly inside her mouth, but Nobu wanted love buoyancy in his novel.

"Half a kg of okra will not last a whole day," he shouted. "Sujata, give me some money to buy more lady's finger."

"Be careful with the currency you spend - money is becoming short these days."

"What happened to the advance money the publisher gave us?" Kalyan demanded.

"You spent the advance money buying a silken shirt, my exhibiting sari, and a fancy cot for Nobu. Don't you remember?"

"I am not spending money for myself only; I am buying things for everyone in this house. You must tell Nobu to finish two chapters quickly so we can ask the publisher for an advance of a thousand dollars."

"I will try my best to explain that to Nobu. Two sections are already completed if you want to take them to the publisher's office…."

Before she finished her sentence, she burped like a lobster because Nobu had kicked the side of her stomach.

"Can you bring the fountain pen and the notebook? Nobu wants to write something down," she asked.

Kalyan brought the notebook and a pen, but her handwriting had stopped after Nobu's kick. In the notebook, the writing implied the novel writing was finished; and Nobu has gone on vacation.

"What is the meaning of that statement? Nobu is still in your stomach, standing upside down. How can he go on a vacation?"

"Nobu said he cannot write now unless two things are settled. First, the money you will receive from the publisher has to be spent on Nobu; second, both of us have to follow Nobu's orders."

"The first question is a legitimate request, but the second question shows too much control," he said.

Sujata continued, "Let Nobu think highly of himself, as if he is the one who is in control, lest he change his mind. The delivery date is in twenty days. Why don't you apply for a loan in the mean time?"

Sadly, Kalyan then went to sleep in the other room. He thought Nobu must be mischievous...but still a genius. He appeared to be as abnormal as his twenty-four fingered maternal uncle!

## Chapter Three

Man thinks one thing, but what happens is another thing.

Eventually, the delivery day arrived. However, there was no one in the house to help; both husband and wife were unscientific fools! After Sujata started experiencing pain every half hour, she realized it was labor pain. Kalyan rushed to a call a taxi – he was only half-dressed!

Sujata was moaning at regular intervals because of the labor pain . To soothe her pain, Kalyan asked her if Nobu, their unborn child, was telling her anything. She told him Nobu was very much afraid; he did not want to come out of her stomach at all!

"That's alright. To lecture an outsider from the stomach is much easier than the goat hunting on the ground."

"You better eliminate all those goat examples from your talk," Sujata said, between breaths. "By teaching all the students in the class, you are watching nothing but goats around you. Nobu is a genius - that you should not forget!"

She was in pain and was talking angrily; she kept rolling back and forth on the bed. Dr. Goswami and an aged nurse appeared as soon as they arrived at the hospital. The nurse was consoling Sujata, telling her to release her stomach pressure slowly. After a short while she said, "You will soon see the reddish face of a newborn child, but do not be afraid because we will be right here."

Now, the labor pains were recurring every fifteen minutes; the pains were shaking Sujata's stomach with a violent seizure. Sujata was still wondering how her son would behave once he was born; she now knew that Nobu was incredibly nervous. He had not found the right time to come from his shell...he was early.

Sujata's ears were ringing with the nurse's voice, "Push, push, push yourself a little harder. You must push a little harder."

Sujata was thinking again that Nobu did not want to be born yet; she was afraid the boy would be very obstinate. She feared he would not be friends with her or the outside world. Before she could think any further, she was shivering violently again with labor pains, and she could hear the nurse's voice telling her to push hard - a little bit more! Sujata realized that Nobu's courage was slowly waning. He was now talking in a very threatening voice, "If you force me to come out so early, you will get the old Nobu, and your novel writing will end!"

"Pressure! Give pressure! Just a little more pressure."

Sujata heard the nurse's voice and realized that Nobu's leg-pinching inside her stomach had nearly stopped. She thought that Nobu would really be a celebrity genius! With him, we will also be famous; the newspaper will publish our pictures, and on TV, they will show us again and again. Most likely, there will be a story written in our honor!

"Give more pressure! Keep pushing," said the nurse.

The doctor added, "You are almost ready to give birth...the baby is almost here!"

Suddenly, Sujata's whole body shook violently, and then her stomach became numb and finally vacant, as if in a dream. She was thinking sluggishly. She was expecting Nobu's voice to forcefully refuse this birth, that he would have started arguing with the doctor. Maybe he would even ask where the doctor kept his bedpan!

With her sleepy eyes, Sujata noticed the doctor was hanging a blood-soaked child in front of her; he was giving the child a mild slap. The baby's mouth started making soft, low sounds. Sujata was afraid Nobu would shout, "You damn, idiotic doctor!"

Sujata was ready for whatever Nobu would say...but he did not say anything. The doctor gave the boy's buttocks two mild slaps again, and the child cried out in a ringing voice. No words from the child, no noisy body shaking. Like any other child, the boy started crying in a sharp, piercing tone.

Sujata was surprised at first; she could not believe what she saw. She did not find anything unusual in Nobu's cry; nothing showed peculiarity in his body or his hand movement. For the previous nine-months, Nobu had bothered her and tormented her so much with his ingenious ideas.

"I thought I was going to be the mother of a genius child and that everyone would appreciate my genius baby. I would be in the audience applauding loudly when Nobu passed his annual examinations in college. He would not be a regular doctor or engineer; he would be as important and as famous as Tagore or Einstein. People would be showing respect to us as if we were celebrities, just like him. There would be no worrying about his career. Everything would come easily to him, the world of happiness would throw open its door to us, and the child would bring us a bigger, better, nobler lifestyle."

Instead of fulfilling all these dreams, she realized he would be like a useless chicken. Her anger and vanity were spread across her dark face, which gave her a peculiar color. In her mental stress, her thoughts were scattering like random leaves blowing in the wind.

With excitement in her voice, Sujata shouted, "Doctor, give the child a few more strong slaps on his buttocks! If you don't, he will remain a crying, insignificant, ordinary man his entire life! He is an ungrateful monkey; he will be a silly mule at best!"

# 4

✦✦✦✦✦✦✦✦

# Aunt from Haiti

*Chapter One*

In the evening, the telephone rang loudly, and when I picked up the phone, a voice filled my ears:

"Brother! This is Sushanta talking - do you recognize my voice?"

I was a little taken aback, but still managed to answer. "You are from the old presidency college, Sushanta Mullick? I am the elder brother of two Sushantas."

"I am Sushanta Halder speaking! While in college, I was two years your junior!"

"Well, what is the news? Where are you calling from?"

"Presently, I am calling from San Francisco. After I moved to New York, I went to Texas and from there to California. I heard you were transferred to the mid-west of America. It's so big - I can't always stay in contact with everyone! Now, I will be sure to stay in touch with you!"

"What is happening with you? Are you coming to this area of the country?"

"Yes, I am! Although I am not just visiting the mid-west - I was transferred to your city through my job."

"Which company are you working for, and when are you coming?"

"I am coming in the first week of January."

"Where will you be staying?"

"For the first few weeks, I will be staying at a hotel. The company has given me a month's expenditure to help me find a new place to live."

"Are you coming with your family?"

"No, they are not coming here yet. My eldest girl is studying in class 10. She would not come here in mid-session but will be here toward the end of August, in grade 11. Meanwhile, the house in San Francisco will be sold; otherwise, buying a house in the new city would cause havoc with our finances."

"Do not think about all these things. Something good will happen with God's wish. Besides, we live in the city. Why are you worried?"

"I am so glad to hear that you are in the city. Otherwise, I wouldn't be able to face all these changes alone."

"Lots of peoples' relatives are here. If you come here with a free mind, everything will work out. One thing you don't have to worry about is your telephone bill because you can use our number as your contact number. Do you understand? Good luck and I will talk with you soon. Bye."

Sushanta was a larger-than-life character who liked to talk and was considered very fickle by other men. He eventually sold his house in California and used the money to purchase a very nice home in the mid-west. His family went to India during the summer time, and Sushanta stayed alone for a month and a half.

During this time, I was visiting Sushanta in his new house. My own wife had gone to my aunt's home in Cleveland to stay for ten days. I could not go with my family, so instead I began to start saving for our next trip to India.

As I relaxed in Sushanta's kitchen, he was telling me what a superb cook he was! But what was the fun in singing one's culinary praise to another temporary bachelor?

After dinner, Sushanta said, "Have a beer and relax. No, wait... now I remember, you do not drink beer, but you always preferred a little hot liquor. Isn't that right? Let's start with a glass of scotch whiskey."

With a half-filled whiskey glass in one hand, I was looking at Sushanta's beautiful new kitchen cabinets.

I said, "Well done on your cabinet purchase; the furniture is immaculate and very stylish."

Sushanta was delighted to hear his friend's praise and told me the furniture was not vine-layered but was made with solid oak wood. "Open the cabinet, you would be amazed."

I opened the cabinet door carefully, and I was shocked to realize that what Sushanta said was true. The cabinets were made of solid oak wood and looked beautiful. By just merely glancing at his cabinets, I saw several brand-new pots and pans. However, at the corner of one cabinet were two ancient-looking saucepans, both of a very black metallic finish.

Although the black pots were washed and cleaned thoroughly, they didn't look brand new; instead, they looked quite outdated and worn. I was surprised to see the two incredibly old pots were kept side by side with brand new pots and pans.

"The old pots belong to you, or did the former house owner leave those?"

Sushanta said in an unpleasant voice, "No brother, those two old pots are mine - someone gave them to me a long time ago."

"Do not get upset. I apologize, my curiosity knows no bounds! Who has given you these old pots? So dark and so well-worn."

"There is a history behind these pots. The pots are fifteen years old. In the days when I was struggling, my aunt from Haiti gave the pots to me. At that time, it was as if the pots were made of gold. Man is an insignificant thing who gets lost in no time."

As he was talking, I could tell the story was bringing back tender memories because Sushanta's throat was choked with emotions, and he stopped talking.

"Brother Sushanta, if these moments are private to you, there is no need to tell the stories. But it seems to me that special memories of your aunt from Haiti and the pots she gave you are worth a time to reminiscence. I don't understand how you can remain so calm."

"Brother, did you not know about my aunt from Haiti? That's not a story from good days but a tidbit from my days of struggling to begin a new life. Would you like to listen to them all? All the personal details?"

"Yes! Yes! I would be glad to listen to your stories of the past. I have been living in America for more than twenty years. To hear stories from your history would be wonderful."

"That's alright, brother. First, let's eat our lunch. Then if you have patience, I will slowly tell you the stories of my aunt from Haiti."

After lunch, we sat around two chairs, face to face with two cups of coffee. Sushanta's eyes were a little sad as his reflected on the olden days - with some love and some stories of struggling.

## Chapter Two

Sushanta's story:

On the TV, you have surely heard of Haiti's president, John Aristid, who left Haiti after his rule in 2004. When he was elected, the new, democratic ruler had to implement democracy.

Before he came to power, the government in Haiti was totally different. At that time, Papa Doc-Duvalier was in power. The torture and turmoil during his rule had wrecked the whole of Haiti from top to bottom. People were fleeing from their houses and running away as fast as they could. Haiti is so small - ten thousand square miles of land – and in that little amount of land, there lived thousands of poor people.

I had left India and had come to America. In America, there was an awful recession, and in Iran, the hostage crisis was critical. I began looking for a job, but I could not find anything. After a lot of searching, moving here and there, I finally settled in the Clinton Arms House in Manhattan, which is sort of a cheap man's accommodation. I stayed in a room which was twelve feet long and eight feet wide. In the bedroom, there was an old bed and a bedspread with pillows. There was an almirah, a writing table, and a chair. I had to share a restroom and a kitchen. Also, we shared a common refrigerator for keeping leftover foods. I started existing on one apple or banana for lunch and a cup of milk with a slice of bread for dinner.

Without a plan, I had come to New York and began to wonder if I had made the correct decision. Sometimes I felt so lonely that I thought of going back to India. Then, my head began to tremble with pain and frustration, I couldn't sleep at night, and I lost twenty pounds. I tried several times to buy tickets so my family could come from Calcutta to meet me in New York. However, I did not have money at hand and receiving letters from my family only made things worse. I felt restless and ended up crying aloud in my room, begging to God to help me survive this darkness. I prayed again and again to find some courage and some food so I could follow a path that would lead to a breakthrough.

Brother, you do not understand how my emotions and my constant hunger affected me. I would walk daily, mile after mile, looking for a job, and when I returned to Clinton Arms, I had to either cook for myself or buy food from outside...all this without any money! I could either eat half-heartedly or remain with an empty stomach; I suddenly realized why poor people sometimes do dishonest, dirty work! My mind was turning like a burnt-out flame.

It was summer, and I decided to go to Trenton for a job interview, which was a distance of seventy miles. When I returned to Clinton Arms at 8 o'clock in the evening, I was downcast because, in the interview, I was asked about my work experience, which I did not have. By the end of the day, I was quite disappointed when I returned to Clinton Arms from New Jersey. I decided to not cook anything that day but to prepare a glass of warm milk instead. However, I did not have any pot for warming, so I wondered what the difference was between drinking milk - hot or cold. None...so I drank raw milk instead, and I began pouring cold milk from a merchant jug into a glass.

I did not notice that a dark-colored woman was observing me from the other side of the kitchen. Suddenly, the old lady started mumbling some unfamiliar words, which I did not understand because she wasn't talking in English.

I said, very calmly, "I do not know what you are saying."

Only God knew what the old lady thought about me. She left the kitchen for a minute, and when she returned, she had a big black pot with a handle and a bottle of sugar.

She said, "Milk should be drunk warm and mixed with sugar."

I still did not understand what she was saying, but from her hand gestures, I realized a little bit of her message. I warmed the milk and drank it slowly from the glass. Very slowly, indeed! I felt a little better after drinking hot milk, so I thanked her for giving me a feeling of contentment.

The old woman noticed how much I was enjoying the milk and sugar, and she quietly smiled after I finished drinking. Then, she started talking again in that strange language. The words she spoke were "Afa, Esprar, Sunsofar," which she kept repeating over and over again. I finally came to know the meaning of the words: "you pet", "hope", and "out of home". I was feeling light-headed, so I mumbled a soft "Thank you" and went to my room.

I met the old lady several times afterward - in the elevator and on the street. Whenever I met her, she always gestured "hello", and I always replied "good morning" or "good afternoon" in return, even though I could not understand what she was saying.

Brother, I told you that I was having a terrible time! Every day I returned to my residence, depressed and feeling quite hopeless. There was no more money in my pocket, I had no food to eat, and I felt absolutely lost and tired whenever I entered the shared kitchen.

One night, the old lady was there cooking rice in hot water. Next to her dinner plate, there were some cooked plantain and some boiled, raw, smelly fish! By seeing the cooked rice and smelling the fish, my stomach started rumbling. The old lady understood my hungry state, and she pulled me by my hands inside the kitchen. Then, she spoke in that same foreign language, and before I knew it, she put a little boiled rice and some plantain on my plate.

While placing some half-sliced boiled fish and some sauce on my plate, she touched her head and stomach, trying to express her feelings. "Eat the rice...infant...if your stomach is satisfied, your mind will also be happy."

The fish began to spread a peculiar smell around the room just like the boiled plantain had done; I have never tasted anything like that. But I did start eating the cooked rice with plenty of hunger. The old woman was nearby watching with her locust-like eyes as I ate the rest of the rice. When I had finished, she added a few lumps of rice from her plate to mine. Again, she said some words in this different language that I did not recognize, but by then, I did understand some of her words by listening to the tone of her voice. It was as if my long-dead mother was standing near me saying, "My son, is your stomach still empty? Will you take rice in your plate again? Would you please?"

I was emotionally upset, and to hide my shame, I ran to the veranda. Brother, can you imagine my condition? A grown man and father of two grown-up children, how could I console myself? Then, I started thinking, "How can I give something to the old woman in return? She is staying in this poor hotel, too; I knew I could find something of value that would let her know of my grati-tude." I searched my mind for what I could give her.

At last, I found a small leather bag among my belongings; it had a fancy drawing on top that had been given to me by my little daughter. I returned to the kitchen with the small gift, where the old lady was still washing our plates. She was surprised when I gave her the gift! No one had ever given her any sort of gift in an awfully long time. After refusing the bag several times, she finally accepted my gift wholeheartedly.

She said, "Merci beaucoup, merci beaucoup." In fact, she was so excited that she touched my head several times in a loving man-ner. Finally, she stood back, looked at me, and she smiled her silent smile.

All of a sudden, an aged black man in dirty clothes entered the kitchen and stood in the middle of the room. After seeing the man, the old woman shouted in an excited voice several words while touching the small leather bag with her fingers. Shortly, her emo-tions cooled a bit, and the man turned to me and said, in broken English, "My name is Andre Desaleon. This woman is pleased to receive your gift. She is thanking you very much."

"She says that you look like her son, and she is asking where you will get your next home-cooked meal. She says you have stayed many days here without eating. If you do not eat, you will quickly become sick, and in no time, your money will vanish into thin air. Why are you making this mistake?" Andre interpreted.

I was surprised to hear all these details through Andre's inter-pretation. I had not realized the woman had seen how often and how little I ate.

Keeping Andre as a middleman, I learned the old woman's name was Meri, and I began to learn a lot about her and about her life.

"What country did Meri come from?" I asked.

Andre hesitantly replied, "We come from Haiti, and we speak the Creole language. Creole is a mixture of classic French and native African languages."

Meri came to me quickly and spoke to me in the Creole language. After a while, she stopped and told me something serious. She wanted to know why I did not cook my meals. She told me rice could be boiled quickly and potatoes or even plantain could be added to the rice. Not eating any food and staying hungry for a long time was very bad.

I explained to her I had come there from India, and I couldn't find any job. In no time, I had become penniless. So, I couldn't even buy cooking utensils.

After listening to me, Andre said, "Why don't you try some odd jobs? What kind of jobs do you know?"

I told him I was a certified accountant; hearing this, Andre was obviously surprised. I wondered if he understood my words correctly. When he told Meri about my education, she placed both hands to her lips and shouted, "Very good, very good," several times.

Then, without speaking again, she left the room but returned after a few minutes. She was holding a Dixie pot of rice, a covered saucepan, and one big spoon. The container must have held four pounds of rice, a few half-seasoned bananas, and some potatoes. She started talking in Creole again - a quick string of random words.

Andre solved my dilemma, "Meri said she wants to give you the Dixie pot, saucepan, and the rice, bananas, and potatoes. Will you please accept these things? She is asking again and again if you will take these things."

I told her I was not a youngster anymore, but Meri was addressing me as her son. What was it she wanted from me in return? What was the real intention behind her kind heart? Finally, I stopped and nodded my head in acceptance. Meri was happy, and she smiled again with that silent smile.

## Chapter Three

After this, through Andre, I learned many things about Meri. She was the daughter of farmers whose house was near the Artibonite River in Haiti. Their only property was a tiny, pudgy plot of land. They survived by fishing and cutting wood sticks in the jungle to sell at Port-au-Prince. Despite the frightening government in Haiti, somehow life had gone on for Meri and her family.

At one point, near her village, there was a hydroelectric power plant being built. In order to accommodate the outside workers who were part of the project near her town, Papa Doc-Duvalier decided to vacate the village and use it for the workers. When the villagers protested the order, they were jailed on a phony charge of stealing.

However, with help from a Voodoo doctor, Meri's family escaped the village. While being smuggled into the US on an overcrowded boat, her husband died due to suffocation and blood dysentery. When they landed, her children left on their own, and she didn't know where they had gone. None of the Haiti immigrants had a visa or passport, and they did not have any money with them. As illegal immigrants, they moved from one state to another like street animals trying to find a place to begin their new lives.

Eventually, Meri disappeared into the crowd of illegal immigrants living in New York City. She worked as a sweeper in a warehouse in the morning. In the afternoon, she worked in an unhealthy, crowded sweatshop where she tailored coats and shirts for poor people. She received only half of the salary that was paid to others, but she couldn't complain to anyone because she was an illegal immigrant. She had not seen her children since they arrived in America, and she didn't know where they were living or if they were well. Somehow, she sent money to her children through a Haitian source, but only God knows what happened to the money. After patiently waiting, she still retained hope that her children were still alive. She believed that she would be able to return to her own native village. She also believed firmly that she would meet with her children somewhere. She was a farmer's daughter who was utilizing her toughness; Meri was strong and carried great hope in her heart.

Why Meri kindly looked at me, only God knows. Her own children were unknown to her for such a long time. Maybe for that reason, she was somehow spilling her motherhood onto me.

During this time, I fell sick for several days, but Meri brought me medicine from the local shops. She begged me to allow her to do this for me, so I did not deny her. I thought that when I became established in my new life, I would help her as best I could. In my mind, I called her my aunt from Haiti. Believing in my aunt's luck, I got my first job interview as a semi-accountant.

"Good luck," she gestured before I left for my first day of work. She was so happy to hear the news of me getting my first accounting job that she called everyone she knew and told them of my good news.

The other members of the Clinton Arms House thought that the old lady had lost her mind! Otherwise, why would she show such sympathy for an Indian foreigner? She bought herself a cheap, two-dollar bottle of champagne and shared it with all the people she knew. She began telling me I would grow more; hope brings more hope, she told me. She also told me it was time to bring my family to America.

From then on, whenever I met her, she would say, "Do not spend your money carelessly. Save more and save plenty. When you will have a house to live, will you keep me as your housekeeper? I will keep your home clean for a very little amount of money. I also work in a tailor shop, so I will do the sewing for your daughter and your wife."

She went on talking at random; I did not understand half of what she was saying. It was as if Meri was dreaming most of the time as she quietly rearranged my household in her mind.

During Easter, my father-in-law sent me some colored shirts as a gift. The gifts contained little things like pictures of my little daughter and shirts made of orange and red colors. I knew that Caribbean islanders love deep-colored clothing, so I decided Meri should wear the orange-colored shirt the next day, and I would ask Andre to photograph her.

As she was getting ready for her picture, I started showing her the photographs of my young children. Seeing the pictures, Meri stiffened, but she looked at the photos again and again with love in her eyes. After kissing the photos several times, she started crying profusely. I did not understand where her emotions had come from because, up until that day, I had never seen a teardrop come from her eyes. While crying, she took her handbag and pulled out an old picture. Due to constant handling, the picture had become dirty and soiled, but despite the dirt on the picture, I could clearly see three small, dirty youngsters - a girl and two boys. Meri couldn't stop crying and kissing the photograph – mumbling softly to herself. Then, she ran from the kitchen; I realized the mistake I had made by showing her the picture of my children. Over time, she had begun to forget about her children, but the photos of my children had abruptly torn away her protective facade.

Basically, in her motherhood, there was a yearning for her own children; she had been sleeping like an old mama bear. All of a sudden, after waking from her hibernation, that protective mama bear surfaced, longing for her children.

In Haiti, there was still plenty of trouble going on. The news came to us that Papa Doc-Duvalier had been overthrown and killed suddenly. The island of Haiti was now taken over by a new military dictatorship. In one aspect, the killing continued; on the other hand, there were those who supported the new leader's unreasonable propaganda. The military management through TV, newspapers, and radio were continually telling the world that all political prisoners would be released from jail in no time and that all the refugees could return to Haiti without any fear. Everyone wanted to rebuild a new Haiti. How far the propaganda had spread, only God knows.

However, the propaganda had spread to New York City, and everyone was a believer. In the Clinton Arms House, there was an increase in the Haitian population and in Voodoo activities. In Haiti, the smell of gun powder and gun fighting were still in the streets. For quite some time, Haiti and Meri were coming back into the public eye.

Andre told me that Meri had gone to a Voodoo center and had come back very late to the Clinton Arms. Her body was shaking violently because of the kind of drug she was given. Two or three times she raised her finger in a kissing-style and went quietly to her room. I didn't realize that was the last time I would see her...my aunt from Haiti was lost forever.

The next day was Friday and coming from work took a little extra time. Putting rice in hot water, I thought that I would go out for an evening walk. While cooking, my roommate showed me that Meri's Dixie pot and her saucepan were lying on the kitchen table. I was surprised to see her old pot lying there, but I noticed a piece of paper underneath the pot. There was something written on the paper, so I turned it over, and I could see it was from Meri because it was written in broken English – "Me, Luv yu, Meri."

I immediately knocked on her door but got no reply. After inquiring about her through Andre, I was told that Meri had not returned from her workplace. It was at that point that I knew my aunt from Haiti was gone. I ran everywhere in the building looking for her but found nothing. I ran to the Haiti general councilor but received no information. I wrote to the Human Rights Association; no reply came. Did Meri go back to Haiti, or was she still looking for her children? I did not know. Poor people are always losing their lives like this; many significant historical facts gobble up the poor peoples' stories. And whoever takes the time to keep track of their collection of memories?

## Chapter Four

The lifetime of a man or woman is a tiny thing, and their stories can get lost so easily. But brother, look at these two aluminum pots; they are still here. They are metallic and sturdy, not lost or broken after many uses. Their outside is black and old, but the inside remains shiny and new. I like to think that my aunt is still living after all. The aluminum pots are dead and dull but not to me. Even today, if I open the Dixie pot, I will hear her timid voice, "espoire, espoire" - do not lose your hope, do not lose your hope; "bon-neor, bon-neor" - be happy, be happy, be well. Though Aunt Meri is lost forever, her love and emotion is kept alive within those two old pots. If love dries out, the household utensils can remain idle. Even if it's written in broken English, "Me-Luv-yu--- Meri."

# 5

┻┻┻┻┻┻┻

# Sound Wave

The universally recognized psychiatrist, Dr. Mitra, walked toward his chambers in the hospital. It was Sunday, but he came to the hospital due to an urgent call from the police chief. They needed the doctor to examine an American engineer who had just been arrested. After his diagnosis, the police would determine what should be done with the criminal. For the time being, the suspect was being kept in an isolated room in the jail, but the police would bring him to the hospital by 8 o'clock that morning.

The hospital was a medium-sized building with an emergency room and an outpatient department. Down the hallway, there were other medical divisions - neurology, pulmonary, cardiology. The mental health division was in a separate wing on the east side of the hospital. Dr. Mitra was a well-respected physician; that is why his administrative office was on the elite west side of the hospital.

So, every day, he had to travel from the east side of the hospital to the west side, and now he was going back to the east side to his private office. Outside his office, there was a hallway and a registration room for patients.

When he reached his office, he was struck by the noisy sounds of the patients - like a harsh morning song. By the side of his office, someone was loudly playing Michael Jackson's song, Bad. The long line of patients was standing around the registration desk, and the relatives of the patients were loitering aimlessly.

A hippy-type, college student was dancing by himself in the middle of the room; he seemed to have forgotten he was in a hospital. On the other side of the reception area, you could hear the noise of driving cars and lorry loads coming from the distant street. You could also hear the rolling train's wheels on the tracks and the buses passing by, full of passengers. All these sounds blended together into one – the patients' painful, roaring cries and the traffic outside...it was deafening!

Dr. Mitra was a busy man, but because he had become accustomed to these daily noises, the sounds didn't bother him. His mind was full of city noises that were continuously created by others. There were only two classes of people in the city: first-class people who have money in their pockets and second-class people who do not. Both groups of people make noises – but in totally different ways.

With quick steps, Dr. Mitra entered his office and greeted his secretary, Namita Sarkar, who said, "Good morning, sir."

As soon as the doctor entered his room, his telephone began ringing. Dr. Mitra asked Namita to bring his daily appointment book before he settled down to answer any phone calls. As he picked up the phone, he heard the voice of his wife. She said, "Today we have an invitation to visit friends. Please return home as soon as you are finished with work; otherwise, they will think we do not want to visit and that we are too self-absorbed."

"I can't leave without finishing my appointments," said Dr. Mitra. "Then, afterward, I have a police case waiting for me; I will try to return home on time, but..."

After he finished his call, Namita came into his room and told him the police-held prisoner had already arrived. "You have to go now to the west side of the building, sir. Here is your appointment list," she said.

Dr. Mitra came out of his room with the list, and as soon as he opened the door, the noises started howling in his ears!

Soft music from the radio was wafting through the room; the distant train added more noise as it rolled down the tracks. In the corridor, there were two people dancing to the young student's random music. There was a thundering of footsteps in the registration office, patients were clamoring for help, and a child that was sitting on an adult's lap was crying loudly because he wanted his milk.

The red light, which signified someone was about to enter, went on as soon as Dr. Mitra entered the prisoner's chamber. The communication boom sounded rudely, and the prisoner was brought into room No. 8. As soon as he entered the room, a loud, clear voice trembled in his ear.

"Good morning, Dr. Mitra," the prisoner said. "I'm sure you will find nothing out of the ordinary by examining me."

Dr. Mitra laughed quietly and thought to himself how every patient says the same thing before being examined. He looked at the corner of the prisoner's eyes and noticed that strangely, the prisoner did not look desperate or anxious. He looked smart and refined; his laughter had a feeling of life and energy. His manners were of a prominent nature, and he didn't seem like a mad man.

In a quiet voice, he addressed the prisoner. "Look here, you are currently a psychiatric patient; based on my report, you need to be examined further. You cannot hide anything from me, so whatever is on your mind, please feel comfortable sharing with me."

As he spoke, he realized the room had suddenly become quiet. The prisoner, with a smile on his face, asked the doctor, "You must be wondering why the room suddenly became quiet - what just happened?"

He laughed, "I have disabled your beeper and sent it to the graveyard; it cannot tell any more lies about me. I have broken your beeper so badly that, without the help of a technician, you won't be able to ever use it again!"

Dr. Mitra suddenly wondered if he had been wrong – was this patient indeed violent?

The prisoner, reading the doctor's mind, replied calmly, "No, I am not a violent person – well, at least when the noise level is below 80 decibels. When any electronic instrument starts producing sound over 80 or 90 decibels, that is when I become violent! You do know that normal talk between humans is usually only 40 decibels. Even if someone shouts loudly, the sound does not cross 50 decibels. However, trains and the lorry load sometimes blare at 80 decibels or more; how can I tolerate that noise?"

Before he finished talking, the radio intercom sounded in their ears. The prisoner jumped onto a chair, pulled the loudspeaker out of the wall, and pulled out the wires attached to it. The radio stopped at once, and the wires became jumbled up awkwardly in a pile on the carpet.

By that time, Dr. Mitra finally understood the behavior pattern of the prisoner. He glanced quickly at the police report to confirm his suspicions.

He said, "You are the famous Mr. Fighter. We have not been introduced formally, but I have heard you are determined to stop all noise pollution. You think you are an expert on the subject."

Mr. Fighter smirked and told him the nickname, Mr. Fighter, had not been his idea; the name had been given to him by the newspaper reporters who covered his stories. He rose from his chair and proceeded to walk toward the doctor and said, "Do not be afraid."

Before the doctor knew what was happening, the prisoner snatched his wristwatch, put it inside his mouth, and started chewing! Like a nut sandwich, he broke the watch with a mild, crunching sound and returned it to the doctor.

"Dr. Mitra, I am personally not angry with you, but I couldn't stand the ticking sound from your watch, and I knew the alarm would go off any minute."

Somehow, Dr. Mitra controlled himself and said, "Mr. Fighter, who has given you the authority to break other people's property like this?"

"The people who have given me the right to break your watch are those who do not sleep at night but loudly play music over their loudspeakers instead. Do not worry; I will replace your wristwatch with a brand new one." He then started singing, "If you do not get grief, how can you rectify things that are wrong?"

Dr. Mitra was surprised to hear Mr. Fighter's excellent singing voice. "Listen, do not create any more trouble. Instead, tell me everything you did before you were caught by the police."

"First of all, I strangled my telephone. I ripped out all the wiring and threw the phone in the dust bin."

"A telephone is a beneficial instrument of society; people are eager to own their own telephone," the doctor interjected.

"In the beginning, I also thought the telephone was a very essential possession in one's daily life. However, the cost of making a phone call has gone up tremendously! There seemed to always be a crossing of phone lines, and you could hear everyone's conversations; you could frequently hear the love talk, or the conversation of some grandma who was looking for some medicine for her granddaughter who had dysentery."

"Besides the telephone, what other instruments have you destroyed?"

"Well, I took our TV set, knocked it out with some hammer blows, and sent it to TV paradise."

"TV gives ordinary people some lively entertainment, doesn't it?"

"But the new-style entertainment is not Bengali-style; it is the so-called new-Hindi cinematic style. First, you watch a boxing match; then, you see young people dancing wildly in crazy, new-style clothes!"

"That's okay; I can see you have an incredible sense of hearing. After you attacked the TV, you struck again - so which instrument did you attack next?"

"I attacked the house intercom system next. I was quietly reading a good book when all of a sudden, I heard my wife's harsh voice over the intercom. "All the cooked rice is stuck together like a snowball. Ugh...it looks so rotten!" After my wife went to bed, I poured a cup of hot tea on top of the intercom. I heard a "bloop" sound, and the next thing I knew, the fuse exploded!"

"Then, when your wife realized what happened, what did she do?"

"She yelled and thought I was crazy!"

"What other mischief have you instigated?"

"Nothing that was not deserved! I have shoved ice cream into my car radio to put it to sleep. In the tourist bus, I tried to lock and scramble the frequency of the radio."

"You certainly know a lot about technical issues. By any chance, are you a professional engineer?"

"You have guessed correctly. Without the brain of an engineer, professional gadgets are a totally useless creation."

"What did you do to the radio inside the tourist bus?"

"The tour was supposed to end in the Ganges near the Kali Temple. I thought that I could sit alone there, with no noise pollution, around the Ganges. Then, I heard one of the passengers shouting that his stock market share of Dalmia Cement was going down."

"What did you do then?"

"I took a scrambler machine and jammed the radio frequency. The news of the stock market was suddenly stopped and ran in a Bear market; it was a very chaotic scene! People were scattering in every direction and running without stopping – just to get away from the bus and from me."

"The police then captured you, correct?"

"Yes! The police captured and arrested me because of everything I had done, even though all was completed with an open hand and an open mind."

"On the complaint sheet, it says the police were called due to the noise on the bus and the chaos that followed for all the passengers. The police said your actions had nothing to do with your ganja or opium, so they thought you would be better off in jail."

"Before the tour bus incident, I invented something new, which is capable of producing above 80 decibels; it is triggered by merely hearing the sound."

"But why have you invented a weapon? You are an engineer, and you took the law into your own hands. You could have gone to court to stop noise pollution, or you could have formed some type of organization dedicated to stopping this noise problem."

"I have tried those solutions, but my wife says that it is useless. My neighbors have laughed at me because I am the minority; I am the only person who is upset about this travesty. Before all this happened, I solved the world's hunger problems; now, I am tackling the problem of noise pollution. But it is an up-hill battle because Bengalis these days like everything loud...loud talk, loud music, and even loud, flashy clothes!"

The doctor pressed further, "Tell me about your new invention; how does it know where the target is without even seeing it?"

"In the middle of the night, whenever people start shouting and interrupting my sleep, I begin to utilize this weapon in order to kill people."

"Have you killed before?"

"First, I killed all the boom boxes I could find. Then, after planning carefully, I started killing everything in my sight.

"In the beginning, I had to practice using this new weapon. If I heard a sound near my house, I would hide behind a corner so I wouldn't be seen, and I would use a mirror to find the offender. Once I knew where the noise was coming from, I would throw a rotten tomato or rotten egg at the person where they would immediately fall to the ground. When this happened, the boom box dropped, and it was killed instantly.

"After this preliminary trial, my aim was so good that I no longer needed the hand mirror to find the culprit. I could guess from which direction the sound was coming before I even took a shot. Within three months, I had the routine perfected; you could hear a pin drop when I was in the street."

"If your techniques were that quiet, how did the police find and capture you?"

"I thought that all culprits had left my area of the neighborhood, but I did not know about the bad lad, Harry. This lad is a troublemaker to the core. He uses hemp and cocaine; he was jailed for six months on a previous charge. However, immediately after his jail term, he started walking the streets, randomly playing his big boom box with the sound unbelievably loud. His boom box was howling at double-speed with the loudest treble I have ever heard! He was friendly with the local political parties; that is the reason the police did not want to arrest him or touch him at all."

"What did you do then? Was his death by a rotten tomato or a poisoned egg?"

"After watching him for two days, I concluded that he was a tough man. I finally took aim with a rotten lime, and it hit him awkwardly under his right eye. The lad had to be in the hospital for two days because of it; those were the days there was finally peace in our neighborhood.

"However, the members of the political party came and told the police all about me and my attack strategies. Of course, the police did not have to force me to talk; I told them everything voluntarily. I thought noise pollution should be controlled, and the movement had to be started by somebody. At first, they thought I was an armed man, so that is why they put me in jail. They will have to release me at some point. In the meantime, I will stay peacefully in their isolated cell."

After talking to me and explaining his story for more than an hour, Mr. Fighter lit a cigarette and raised it to his mouth. The rule was "No Smoking" inside the private office of a doctor, but Dr. Mitra did not object. If the patient felt comfortable, there was no pressure placed upon him and he could act freely.

"Mr. Fighter, shouldn't your job of noise pollution control be done by responsible, government officials?" the doctor mused.

"Look, the public is busy earning their daily bread; in the meantime, the responsible, honest politicians have vanished. The government has become very callous toward its citizens, so I have to take this on myself."

He started singing, "If nobody hears you protest, then you go alone." He began laughing loudly.

"It seems you are willing to spend a little time peacefully inside the jail."

"Let me stay for two weeks, at least," he pleaded. "The longer I stay in jail, the more people will know about the problems surrounding noise pollution."

After talking with the doctor, Mr. Fighter suddenly became very emotional and said with an excited voice,

"Doctor, you are a politician. When your type earns money and prestige in life, you no longer think about the ordinary people on the street. By that time, you can buy anything that makes you happy. The war I am fighting is against you and the politicians; there should be a revolution among the people.

"The radio, which has ice cream in its mouth, will say I am just a passing trend.

"Well then, doctor, you better send me to jail for the time being. At least there I can stay peacefully for a few more days."

"If that's what you want, then I can recommend it, but now, my session with you is over. I have no further questions to ask you, and I can start writing your report."

"You can do whatever you feel is right, doctor. One thing you must mention is that I am not a mad man. Over the last forty years,

I have maintained a happily married life. I have collected some secret cotton balls in my pocket, so if anybody cries above 80 decibels, I can put the cotton in my ears, and no one will harm me. Now let me go and think about a mad man like me, and I will say goodbye."

The doctor rang for the attendant, and the policeman came and took Mr. Fighter away.

The noise of the lorry, the political slogans, the patients' loud murmurs, and sounds like hyenas were outside in the hallway. Now, with the opening of the door, the hyena uproar spread freely.

The police chief asked, "Dr. Mitra, what is the diagnosis of the patient?"

"He's a little disorientated, and he can't tolerate loud noises; basically, he is not violent at all. Seems to have a very friendly attitude."

"What is the prognosis?"

"Indefinite...we have to watch him more. I will submit my report by this afternoon. Now, you must keep him inside that lonely cell for at least three more days."

At last, Dr. Mitra returned to his eastside, private office. The hallway was still roaring violently with patients' pathetic crying mixed with gut-wrenching music. On the street, there were the rumbling sounds of lorries, trains, and buses. Today, Dr. Mitra's primary air conditioner was making a peculiar noise as if it were throwing a tantrum; the ambulance of the hospital started reving its motor before picking up more patients. A disorientated taxi tried to overtake a slow, public transport bus.

Dr. Mitra thought in this mad world, his mind was being tortured with all the commotion. Where and when will the patients regain their senses?

He entered his secretary's office and started listening to the morning radio program. Suddenly, an announcement from the hospital intercom floated into the air, "Will the parents of a missing child come to the front desk? Your son has been found wandering the hallways, and we would like to reunite him with his family."

How did his secretary complete her daily work in this noisy atmosphere? The doctor was wondering how he could get away from Mr. Fighter, at least for the time being, without him reading his mind and hearing his feelings.

The man has to live within the sound around him, and there is noise everywhere. Now, what medication could he give this patient? Should he bring the patient into this clattering atmosphere, or should he treat the patient first with medication? No, he should try both methods, he decided.

The telephone suddenly rang like a drum beating in his head. Again, the noise started...telephone – intercom - drum beating; telephone – intercom - drum beating. Even on Sunday, the noise monsters were working ferociously!

Dr. Mitra was no longer a psychologist; he was slowly becoming a mental patient. In the city, it seemed as if every mad man was reaching for him, grabbing him. His private office was the only place he could feel at peace; it was his only safe Heaven. He hurried inside his private office and shut the door.

Usually, he slammed the door with a loud noise. Today, he did not do that; as a mental patient, he started looking all around. Then slowly, very slowly, he closed his door. If he didn't proceed with caution, Mr. Fighter would hammer him with his weapon - that sound-evading tomato - like he did with those boisterous people on the street. And hearing that noise pollution, all the men of the city would giggle at him with high-pitched laughter. The flower was blooming within the garden, and the noise it was making sounded like a mild bomb explosion. God save the flower; God save the man...

# 6

~~~~~~~~~~

# The Turtle Man

Manab had always believed that a turtle was a bad omen; something to be avoided. If he saw a turtle on his way to work, he knew he would have a terrible day; that is the belief of most typical Bengalis. The idea of a turtle bringing bad luck was difficult for Americans to understand. To them, a turtle was a valuable possession. When I asked my American friends why the idea of a turtle being a bad omen is so foreign to them, they could never give an answer. They just shrugged their shoulders and laughed. A turtle cannot give an answer to this question either because they are truly a dumb animal, and of course, they don't have the power to decide a person's fate.

Manab Mitra was a philosophy teacher; his co-worker, an American professor named John White, was a firm believer that a turtle can predict whether his day was going to be good or bad. John also invested a great deal of money in the stock market. That is why, every day before he left his apartment, he would place his domesticated turtle on the lowest step of his staircase, waiting patiently to see what the poor turtle would do.

The stairs to his porch had four steps total. As John watched, he knew if the turtle began to wiggle and to climb the stairs back to the top, then he took that as a good sign. He felt this was an indication that the stock in which he was investing would surely go up in value. If he noticed the turtle was sitting there like a lump with a callous look on his face, then John knew his stock would probably go down, and he would lose money. The peculiar thing is that most of the time, John continuously made money in the stock market... he never seemed to lose!

John had told Manab about his turtle and about how it seemed to be able to predict the future. Manab was from India and felt John's winnings were most likely explained by the Law of Probability; however, he didn't immediately dismiss John's ideas either. Could there be some truth to this idea?

One day, Manab and John had completed the day's classes and were walking outside on the school's campus. When they were close to 16th Street, John exclaimed, "Mitra, tomorrow is your birthday! I want to give you a gift in celebration – will you please accept my gift?"

Mitra did not protest and smiled instead with a look of appreciation. He followed John into a nearby store where there were many birds hanging in cages from the ceiling and several fish aquariums against the wall with all kinds of odd creatures swimming in a slow dance.

When the shop owner saw John, he smiled broadly, "A new kind of turtle has just arrived. Would you like to see it?"

Then, he looked at Manab and said in a low voice, "You know a turtle is a good luck charm."

He cautiously took the turtle from the aquarium and placed it in John's hand. Manab noticed the turtle was not very big – in fact, it was quite a small creature. The turtle's shell was a shiny black color sprinkled with many peculiar-colored spots.

The shopkeeper again said, "Buy it now! Soon good luck will smile upon you. I promise!"

John nodded his head and paid the man as the shopkeeper showered the tiny turtle with many kisses. He gently placed the turtle in a paper bag and handed it to John who immediately sang out, "Happy birthday to you, Manab, and I hope many more will come."

He handed the turtle to Manab, and as was his habit, he hesitated at first. Then, he smiled and gladly accepted this unique birthday gift.

Manab was a professor of philosophy, so he was used to pondering and analyzing all new situations. If buying a turtle could change one's luck, then why didn't everyone buy turtles instead of lottery tickets? This was an escapist theory – and who ever said that Americans do not believe in escapism?

Their walk back to the campus was a quiet one, and when they arrived at the school, they said their good-byes and went their separate ways. The turtle was moving and scraping inside the paper bag, but in the busy New York City streets, no one noticed his package. Manab was excited to show his daughter and his son his new gift; he knew they would break into laughter at the antics of the silly creature.

No...that did not happen.

When he walked in the door, he received no greetings, not a sound. So, he quickly took the turtle out of the bag and put it on the carpeted floor for his children to see. From a distance, the turtle didn't look like any kind of living animal; it seemed to be nothing more than a small, checkered stone. With a smile on his face, Manab looked at his children expecting a reaction; however, they both stood still in the corner, no movement, staring at him as if he had lost his mind.

The feeling in the room was cold and judgmental; their faces were a mirror of their mother's face – odd and uninspiring. Manab hid his feelings and thought maybe the gift of a luxurious Mercedes Benz from their grandfather was the reason they responded so coolly. Maybe this gift paled in comparison to Grandfather's lavish present.

Joy and Joyita, after a few indifferent stares, observed the turtle for a moment. He knew they wondered why their father had placed a filthy, little turtle on their clean white carpet. Watching his children's faces, Manab sat up with a faint smile on his lips.

At first, he thought he would explain the animal was nothing to be afraid of and that it could bring good luck to them. He would tell them they could play with the pet to occasionally give it a little freedom. They would not have to ask permission, just play with it. Manab really thought the children would play with the turtle once they got used to it, and he would be able to share their laughter and enjoyment. He crossed his legs awkwardly and said to the turtle, "Mr. Turtle, will you move your body a little bit and ask my children to sit and play with you? Prove to them this in not a haunted house where little children are forbidden from laughing and having fun!"

He thought this would make his children laugh and join in the fun; instead, he was not prepared for what happened next. His son, Joy, walked up to the turtle, and with his foot, pushed the turtle over and onto its back! The turtle looked startled and began waving his little legs in the air. It was desperately trying to push himself right-side up. Manab thought his daughter, Joyita, would surely help the distressed creature back on its feet, but she stood silently and didn't move – just like her brother. It seemed as if they both wanted the turtle to lay there on the carpet and continue his struggle. He realized now that they thought this filthy animal was nothing more than a cheap plaything cast aside in an alley.

Manab was crushed after observing his children's rudeness. Still sitting on the floor, he helped the turtle back to its feet. The turtle seemed to give him a faint smile as if saying "thank you" and stood completely still, never moving from the spot. At first, he blamed society for influencing his children's choices – always thinking of themselves over others. In India, he had come from a household of an ordinary family...he did not like the audacity of humanity here in America. Eventually, he quietly absolved this self-ish culture and blamed himself for accepting the gift from John in the first place. Is a man's luck really spinning like a wheel, or does it turn abruptly by the wistfulness of others?

Manab sometimes lacked ambition. Sometimes he thought an occasional gift of money from his family would bring happiness to his home. Sometimes he felt a feeling of satisfaction in a life well-lived would create a truce between his wife and himself. That is why he was afraid to live close to his father-in-law's family. That is why he did not object to marrying Jayanti, who was far more superior than Manab when it came to money and social status. What he truly feared was their expensive townhouse in New York City and the Mercedes in their driveway; both luxurious gifts from his father-in-law.

Still, his modest income as a college professor was reasonable. He was not totally compliant or controlled by his wife, which would have caused incredible internal strife. Manab was a student of philosophy, so from many angles, he tried to analyze himself and the life he was living.

For example, yesterday while he was taking a shower, he scrutinized his entire body again and again. He was already in his forties, but what he saw puzzled him. Everyone was born with the same features and with the same demands of daily life; if he were to look inside his body, he would find no difference between his body or that of John or his friend, Harry. How could he have expected his body to stay the same after living so many years? The water was flowing over his body slowly, and his profile in the window was distorted by the slanted rays of the sun. Manab suddenly no longer liked the body he saw in the mirror. No! The reality was that Jayanti's coldness toward him had made his body useless!

Alas, if I can keep the light rays steady and strong enough, man's life is not that unimportant either.

So, if the fruit is squeezed one more time, there may be some juice left inside. Otherwise, why would Jayanti's body come so close to his?

Fifteen years had passed since their marriage, most of it had been viewed through a camouflaged fog. As he thought about the silly marriage arrangement with Jayanti, his body began to tense; he could feel his hands and legs stiffen. After the marriage, he thought, being Jayanti's husband, he would be allowed to change her name from Sarkar to Mitra. However, this did not happen.

Stepping out of the shower, he decided he would open all the windows in his house, one by one; he knew a man needed to keep his mind clear – always. He knew a confused mind gradually causes problems within a marriage.

But that did not happen either. Jayanti was the sole dictator of the household. Her behavior was like the queen of the celestial heaven – perfect and extremely polite. She was like a shiny, perfume bottle; the outside looked delicate and sophisticated, but if you handle it carelessly, it will break into a million pieces. There was always a defensive wall between her body and his; however, in the beginning, there was no break in the passion of having two children, one after another. And now, the children were just like their mother – refined and cold-hearted. Even their names – Joy and Joyita – were similar to hers.

Being alone, day after day, Manab eventually became very distraught and depressed. He knew that money controlled many things in life; in America, if a man had no wealth, that meant he also had no social status. He also knew that being a philosophy professor was not very high on the social ladder. Then, there was the distance between his children and himself, which had become very painful. He toyed with the idea of going back to India – with his head down and as a defeated man.

With all these emotions, he felt he was destroying the peace and happiness of his family. He was always afraid that the day would come when Jayanti's understanding of him would disappear and any small mistake on his part would cause the family to crumble. It was this interpretation of his life that made him stand up to Jayanti's behavior and to lose his fear of her.

Jayanti returned to their residence and saw Manab still sitting on the carpet with the sleepy, little turtle – she was not surprised. Standing like a silent child, she stared at him. With her eyebrows slightly tilted, she tried to understand the situation, and then she wrote a few words on a piece of paper and placed it on the floor in front of him. As if one piece of paper had solved the complicated situation, she quietly walked out the door. He watched Jayanti's coming and going and realized she had not been happy with him or with his little turtle.

He read the scrap of paper that she had left. "Decide who you want to remain – the turtle or your family."

Surprised, Manab didn't understand why he needed to make a quick decision regarding this matter. Then, he realized slowly the issue with the turtle was just an excuse. The turtle could leave the house anytime – it was a trifling matter; this could not be the cause of their divorce. The reason for a divorce should be something serious and profound but to keep a turtle in the house is neither. Manab did not want a divorce for any reason; he came from a so-called "renowned Indian family". The paralyzing effect of a divorce did not make any sense to him; he wrote on the back of the note that the turtle would be thrown away, and Jayanti could return home at once.

Remembering that she had taken the family car, he told his daughter he was going for a walk to get rid of the turtle and that her mother could return home.

Removing the turtle from his home was a small matter, but it had been a birthday gift from his friend, John, in order to bring him good luck. He had a wife and two beautiful children – he didn't need any more good luck. So, he opened the door to leave, while his two children stood and stared.

In his hand, he held the paper bag that was carrying one little, innocent turtle. It was beginning to get dark, and Manab tried to decide how to rid himself of this creature. He looked at the sky and decided to head to the city to walk and think for a while. There was always some magic in New York City. The afternoon glow of the setting sun's red rays eventually turned into the blue and red-colored lights of the flashing, neon signs on the buildings.

All of a sudden, the little turtle started moving and scratching in the bag, and he knew he had to decide. He didn't want to dispose of the creature on Park Street, which was too near their house. He was now close to the campus where he worked; he couldn't leave the turtle there. He turned and started walking toward the pet store, but when he found the store front, it had already closed for the day. Well, maybe he could get rid of it somewhere as he went back through the subway; no, the other passengers would notice and would scowl at him. The turtle stopped moving, and Manab thought it must have fallen asleep. How grand it would have been if he opened the bag and the turtle simply ran away – but there was no luck for Manab.

Soon, he found himself at the edge of his college campus again. He noticed a garden path under some trees on campus, and he thought this would be the ideal place to release the turtle! As he stepped over a shrub and some small herb plants, he heard the sound of an approaching car. The man who got out of the car was a policeman, and he was walking directly toward Manab.

"What are you doing in the middle of these shrubs?" the office asked sternly. "Are you urinating and hiding so you won't be caught?"

Ever since the attack of the World Trade Center, people of authority always looked suspiciously toward men from the Middle East.

With a nervous look, Manab forced a smile. He showed the policeman the paper bag and said, "No. This is not a bomb...it is just a poor little turtle."

The policeman didn't laugh or smile; instead, he said in a harsh voice, "Why are you throwing a turtle in the middle of these flowers? Pick up the turtle now."

He tried to explain to the officer that it was a good turtle – nothing more; in fact, it would bring good luck to him every time. After waiting a few minutes in silence, he finally said, "I will give it to you for good luck. Will you please accept it?"

The policeman thought Manab was joking and said sternly, "Keep your turtle in your bag. If your house is on Park Street, what are you doing here on 106th Street? Are you drunk?"

The officer stepped closer to see if he had been drinking. Then, he shouted, "Take this turtle and go home!"

Manab picked up the little turtle, who was sitting very still and not moving an inch, when he thought he should just throw it in front of a moving car. That would have solved his problem!

As he walked, it occurred to him the turtle was just a ridiculous excuse for a divorce; it was not the real problem. And he knew Jayanti would invent some other reason for divorce...maybe tomorrow or the next day or the next. Her excuse might be as trivial as the problem with the turtle, or it might be much stronger. The ridiculous thought of divorcing because of a turtle would not be believable enough for her friends and relatives. He knew she didn't want her reasoning to appear comical; she did not want to be laughed at. Manab decided he would not give Jayanti any additional opportunities to find fault with him and that would stop all talk of divorce. He put the paper bag and the little turtle under his arm and walked resolutely toward his home.

When he entered his front door, the children were in bed, but Jayanti was sitting firmly on the sofa with a queen-like attitude, waiting for him. Her eyes had a haughty, arrogant look, and her mouth was dripping with coldness. Manab, without showing any emotion, sat in front of Jayanti and quietly lifted the turtle out of the bag. He held it directly in front of her; the turtle was like a stone sculpture – no movement whatsoever. The poison from Jayanti's eyes struck him like an arrow; no words came from her mouth. After staring blankly for several minutes, she stood up, turned abruptly, and went upstairs to her bedroom.

After a few minutes, she came back to the living room with a harsh look on her face. Her jaws were clenched and stiff, which gave her face a wide, angular appearance. With her calculated movements, she walked to the door, turned, and said, "You will not have to wait for very long. You will receive papers from my attorney shortly."

She closed the door with a loud bang...she was gone.

The turtle had not moved a muscle since Manab had taken him out of the bag; instead, he sat on the carpet like a silent, stone chip. As Manab watched, the turtle started to change. It was as if the creature had been listening to Jayanti's angry words and had clearly understanding every word she had uttered. His four tiny feet came out from his shell and began to wave around in the air. Then, his soiled little nose peeked out of the shell, and his neck followed like a clumsy mermaid. He started shifting his bulk from right to left, left to right, in a systematic way. Was he trying to walk or was he trying to dance?

In this elegant, refined drawing room, Manab's turtle seemed to enjoy the rhythmic movements. As he moved closer, he swore he saw a wry expression on the turtle's face. The turtle looked Manab in the eyes and smiled as if to say, "Oh! Manab, your luck has slowly and steadily come to the surface! Now is the time for you to dance, too, for your luck has just changed for the better."

# 7

⤙⤙⤙⤙⤙⤙

# Grover Snyder

*Chapter One*

The Delaware River was about half a mile away, the riverside was divided by a series of poplar trees, and the western side was dark like a red rose with the sun was slowly grazing the sky. Subrata walked across the park at this time every day. In his memory, lots of old thoughts flashed, and he wished to share the stories with somebody. But Shefali did not accompany him very often for evening walks because in the park, she had to keep an eye on their son, Jigo. That's why walking alone was not to Subrata's liking, but he understood her reasoning.

Subrata was thinking how lucky he was; within two and a half years, he had settled down in America. In the first two years, he and his wife had some difficult times while working odd jobs. After living in America for only six months, Shefali's father died, but the couple couldn't visit their native country to be with family because of their financial troubles. Shefali cried a lot, but she did not blame Subrata for not going to India because Shefali understood their financial troubles as well.

Subrata had come to the city of Burlington only six months prior. Shefali was quickly able to find an odd job, and she supported her husband while he was looking for a job, too. She believed Subrata would definitely find a job in which he would become highly successful.

When Subrata arrived home, his mind was refreshed, and he started singing in his hoarse voice, knowing that everything was right in his world.

In a sing-song voice, he called out, "Sefa, Sefa, where are you?"

Shefali was surprised to see Subrata so happy; she asked what had made him so joyful.

Subrata replied, "You are working an odd job in order to support me while I am working on my career, so you should be rewarded. I will buy you something a little expensive - for our wedding anniversary."

"Whatever you will give me as a gift will be enough for me. Do forget about the expensive gift."

"Give and take is a necessary quality for a successful marriage."

"So, what happens between a couple is not important, but what will happen between the couple in the future – that is most important."

"What you are saying now seems like a puzzle to me; I don't understand what you are trying to tell me."

"Oh, you do not have to understand everything I say. Whatever your intuition tells you, you should agree with. You can do whatever you feel is right on our wedding anniversary."

"All right...then, please arrange to have a beautiful dinner for the two of us. In the evening, we shall enjoy the night fully with lots of fun. Our anniversary will be relaxing and devoted to just the two of us."

Hearing that, Shefali started laughing...

"Okay, I will arrange everything. If the celebration is in our house, we should also invite Grover, right? He has known us for over six months, and still, we have not invited him to visit our home for dinner."

"A marriage anniversary is a private affair. Why would you invite Grover, who is an outsider, to celebrate such a special occasion with us?"

"Grover has done so much for Jigo; he has taken him to his school functions, and he has taken him to various musical events. He has waited at the bus stop for you to come home; he also went to visit you at the hospital when you were sick. Have you forgotten all that?"

"No, my memory is not so bad that I have forgotten. After all, I am an engineer, so my memory is very strong. Why don't we send him a lovely Christmas gift instead?"

"Does sending a Christmas gift repay him for everything he's done for us? Life is not that simple. The old man loves our family, and he would be extremely happy to be included in our wedding anniversary celebration."

"But I feel a wedding anniversary is a private occasion that should be celebrated with family, and I'm sure Grover would not feel slighted if he weren't invited. He would be happy receiving a Christmas gift," Subrata insisted.

"I agree with you – a wedding anniversary is about celebrating the love of two people while being surrounded by close family members. It's an incredibly special time! However, isn't Grover a 'close family member', too? We left our immediate family in India, while Grover has become a part of our lives here in America; he has taken a place in our home as if he was close family. I'm asking you to open your heart to him and to include him in our special evening."

Now, Subrata became very agitated. He asked sternly, "Why do you insist on bringing a foreigner to our dinner table?"

"Did you know Grover had a daughter named Sheli; a name that is so similar to my name? His daughter died at a young age.

"When we first moved here," she continued, "the three of us happened to be in the shopping center at the same time. You called my name, and he thought that somebody was calling Sheli, his daughter's name. That is how we first met him!"

"I clearly remember that incident. The old man was calling you 'Shelly, Shelly', and you were completely overcome with emotions."

"No, not at all. Do you remember the night we all went to the Philadelphia Liberty Park in Grover's car? When Jigo was lost in the crowd, we were all running and looking for him like mad people. This old man ran and called the police who were able to find Jigo at last. Did you forget about that?"

"No, Shefali, I did not forget anything. My memory is not as dull as you think. That old man has done so many things for us, but it's odd they way he does things. For instance, why does he come over here so early in the day to visit? Why doesn't he just pick up the phone and call us instead of coming over? It seems like he is here all the time!"

"He is an old man living alone, and he has no friends. He lost his wife a while ago, and his son is living in Chicago with his wife. He just loves having someone to talk with."

"But why does an old man come to visit so often - without any invitation? When he does this, there is no privacy for either of us."

"Has Grover ever come to our home when you are not here? He is simply a lonely, old man."

"I am not saying that Grover is a suspicious man, but he is not like any typical American I have ever met!"

"Did you know that Grover's older sister lives in the next township in an old house? She is nearly ninety years old, and she very seldom leaves her home. Grover goes to her house daily to visit; he stops at our house when he goes to visit with his sister."

"Grover never told me about his sister. Otherwise, I would visit her myself when I have the time."

"You usually seem to avoid Grover; that is why he never told you about his sister. What about the time he spends talking with

Jigo? The two of them talk for hours! He even listens intently when I talk of my family history. He asks simple questions that show he is interested; like what does my mother like to do in her spare time? He thinks growing older is a curse; he sometimes gets very emotional when we talk. He can be very sensitive sometimes."

Subrata was thinking deeply now that Shefali might be lonely, too; he realized she had been lonely ever since her father died. At first, he felt sorry for her – being alone in America, her family still living in India, and only having Grover for a friend; that must have been difficult for her to bear.

But soon, his emotional thoughts began to fade, and his temper flared again.

He said angrily, "You should stop talking about Grover all the time! I wanted to plan our wedding anniversary, and all you can talk about is Grover, Grover, Grover..."

## Chapter Two

After that day, when Subrata and Shefali further discussed their anniversary plans, there was never again any mention of Grover coming for dinner. However, Grover still came to Subrata's house to visit on a regular basis; between coming and going to visit his sister.

One day, Grover told Shefali that he had seen a small, two-bedroom apartment that he knew was for sale. He thought Subrata and Shefali might like it, too. The price was right, and the kitchen was slightly bigger so that Shefali would have a lot of room for her Indian cooking, which generated a lot of oily fumes of various spices.

Besides that, the house had a small, attached garden where she could grow some Indian vegetables. On the other side, there was also space where she could plant a small flower garden.

In their family's house, Grover told them his daughter used to keep small pots for growing plants. He had been very fond of her beautiful flowers!

Another day, Grover told them in a shallow voice, that there was also space where a small swing could be installed, where Subrata and Shefali could swing slowly.

Grover stopped and started laughing loudly. "Subrata, do you know how much Shefali loved to swing when she was young? One time, she was swinging in the park, and a wild cow came close to her and decided to graze nearby. Shefali, in her childish tenacity, began poking the cow with her umbrella. The cow eventually took offense at her actions and jabbed her arm with its horn! The injury to Shefali's hand caused her to be hospitalized for two days."

Subrata had seen Shefali's scarred hand so many times, but he had never asked how the injury came about. This was the first time Subrata heard the story behind the cut on her hand...and a stranger to the family was the person to tell him the details!

His pride was deeply wounded, and he snapped, "We will not be able to buy the smaller house you told us about; we will use the money to vacation in India instead."

The conversation was quickly diverted from talk of Shefali's scarred hand. Grover felt badly that he had upset Subrata and agreed it was a good idea to go to India to be with Shefali's mother.

In the meantime, Subrata was wondering if he even fully knew his wife. He was afraid that he only partially knew her, especially since a foreigner was the person to tell him her intimate, childhood story. He knew every man and woman carried their own thoughts and memories, but Shefali's mind was cast into two sections; the one section that did not share her childhood story with him, and the other section that did not want to divulge the news. He decided to overlook the conversation and to stay in the darkness for a while.

For the next ten days, they did not see Grover at all. Subrata became worried and asked Shefali if she knew where he was. He said, "I have not seen Grover for a couple of days. Do you know where he's been?"

With a dry feeling in her throat, Shefali answered, "Yes, I do. He is in the hospital. I called there and spoke with a nurse. She told me they think Grover had a heart attack. He has been in the intensive unit for three days; while there, the doctor realized he is suffering from diabetes, too."

After hearing the news, Subrata immediately began to feel guilty, and he decided he would call Grover, when he was released from the hospital, and invite him to their house for a quiet dinner.

After a month's time, Grover reappeared in Subrata's house; to be honest, he looked awful indeed. He spoke very slowly instead of in his usual jovial voice, and his mind seemed to move like a defeated battle commander. He left the house after only a few minutes of small talk. It was after this time that Grover's visits happened less and less. He and Jigo hardly played at all any more.

But Shefali was able to remain calm during his visits. "First of all," she said, "you need to get well quickly. If there is a sick man in the house, the home will not remain happy."

Grover pointed to the big tree next door, and said, "See that tree? Every year it is growing older, but that doesn't affect the tree's energy or liveliness. In the winter, the tree becomes leafless, but come spring, it will be full of flowers. In a man's life, no new leaves ever appear on an old man's body. He must live by waiting for the next generation."

Even if his health didn't permit it, Grover gradually began to increase the number of visits to Shefali's house. In spite of this, the conversations between Shefali and him were not as before. He would sit down and quietly look at Jigo completing his homework. She could tell his weakened health was not the life he wanted to accept.

Shefali became quieter, too, and she told Jigo not to play so roughly with Grover. She tried to remind him to take his medication regularly as the doctor had prescribed. It was in this state that months passed and before they knew it, autumn had arrived.

The leaves on the trees had changed their color from green to yellow to red. It was on a night like this that Grover sat in the house for a long time without saying a word. He studied Shefali as she observed her Puja ritual of praying to God. He also watched her lighting the Puja candle, and he quietly observed how she cooked the Indian vegetables.

The clock on the wall showed it was 6:30 pm, and Grover slowly stood up because it was time for him to go home. Shefali called Jigo so he could say goodnight to Grover, and then performed her daily ritual of reminding Grover to take his medication and to carefully return home.

"Promise me," she said again and again.

Finally, Grover took Shefali's hand in his. After looking at her face for a very long time, Grover said, "Man's life, career, marriage, everything is like a battlefield. You cannot win every war."

Then, looking at Shefali's face very slowly, Grover started singing in a weak but cracked voice:

"You've got to give a little, take a little, and let your poor heart break a little. That's the story of, that's the glory of love."

"Good night Shelly, good night Subrata, good night my sweet boy, Jigo. Good night everybody."

The wary smile had returned to his old lips - these were Grover Snyder's last words in Subrata's house. Grover died peacefully two days later. The house remained, the city remained, and the memories remained, but the man vanished quietly from their lives. Called by some supernatural distance, Grover did not wait for a dinner invitation from Subrata.

## Chapter Three

First of all, it was Subrata who got the news of Grover's death. Shefali had gone to the park with Jigo for his afternoon play time. Subrata thought he should not delay telling her the sad news, so he told her immediately when she returned home. When he informed her of what had happened, her face clouded over; with no speaking or crying, she went upstairs and tightly closed the bedroom door behind her. The evening slowly proceeded, and the entire house gradually dipped into cold black darkness - nobody spoke.

Shefali remained silent for the next two days; she did not talk to anyone, neither did she go to her work. She did not cry at all - not a single teardrop fell from her eyes. She did not speak Grover's name, and this puzzled Subrata. He thought Shefali was trying to understand her feelings and she would eventually be fine, so he left her to her thoughts.

Grover's funeral was the following Saturday. They were informed about the funeral date by his son over the phone, in addition to receiving a funeral invitation. Grover's daughter-in-law came from Chicago, and everything was beautifully arranged.

When Subrata told Shefali of the date of the funeral service, she refused to go. Subrata was surprised. "What is the matter with you, Shefali?" he asked angrily. "Grover loved you so much, and you will not go for his funeral? Is that the correct way to show one's respect for someone?"

"I knew Grover when he was a well man – while he was filled with life and funny stories – let me keep that image in my mind. I refuse to see his shriveled body with his colorless mouth! I do not want to see him like that!"

"Still, it is only proper for you to pay respect to him one last time."

"When he was alive, we did not honor him by inviting him to our home for dinner. What use is it to respect a dead man? When my father died, I did not show any respect to him either."

Shefali's hardened face stopped Subrata from going any further; he felt she was being very cruel. When Grover was alive, she spent hours talking to him, and now that he was dead, it seemed as if she had totally pushed him out of her mind. Such a strange world...as an engineer with a mathematical and logical mind, he couldn't understand her.

Subrata tried to reminisce with Shefali by mentioning Grover several times. Grover had fixed this door knob, Grover loved to eat salad as raw food, Grover slipped and fell down the staircase with Jigo last year. Subrata could not forget all of these things. How could Shefali have forgotten him so quickly?

In spite of his insistence, Shefali did not attend Grover's funeral, and Subrata had to go alone. He bought an expensive flower bouquet and signed "Shefali, Jigo, and Subrata" on the card. There Grover's son met him and told him his father talked about them frequently.

Several days passed and all of a sudden, Shefali asked Subrata about her father's ritual death anniversary. "This time, father's death anniversary will be offered here by me. I want you to create a well-organized celebration by bringing in a professional Indian priest; R. Bhattacharya is the priest whom I saw visit in New Jersey. If you call him personally, he will come - if he gets his fee paid in full. The anniversary celebration will finalize my father's death and will allow everyone to feel closure to his passing."

Subrata did what he had to do for his family's happiness.

## Chapter Four

After calling different locations, Subrata announced a firm commitment with R. Bhattacharya as the priest for the occasion. He collected the sacred Hindu-style utensils for prayer; that means he collected the paddy, bailey grain, dried Tulsi leaf, and copper-made Puja utensils, and the priest had everything he needed for conducting the religious service. For charity purposes, he needed the loincloth, the bronze-pots, towel, etc., and the priest brought everything else from Calcutta.

The day of the celebration, Shefali took her bath early in the morning and wore a red-bannered sari, the female cloth. She fasted without drinking water; the priest explained the things that needed to be done in an annual funeral celebration.

First was the establishment of Brahman, which was followed by the opening call ceremony, the gift of the ceremony, and so on. After that, the rice-pass, the fire semesis, and lastly, main-ere initiation of fire. The priest told Shefali to write the full names of relatives on your mother's side and father's side of the family. Before uttering any hymn, she would have to speak with the tribunal mind (Gotra) of that Lord. Her father's surname was Chatterji, so he must be of Kashyap Gotra. In the start, she had to be positive about the person's name and Gotra. She could not forget it.

The priest first started the ceremony with Brahmana hymn "oum-Darbhomoy-Brahmana vo namo". Then, he told Shefali she should sit on the north side and put water to Brahmana. Then, she should tell your father's side of the family that everyone should chant, one by one "oum pattin...", and she should put water in his name.

The ceremony continued, and even during the uttering of the father's side hymn, Shefali was hungry but never shaky. While she was adding the last rice offering to her father's name, she began to cry.

Men and women's feelings are like locked lakeside water; water always tries to find an empty hole through which it can flow outside.

Gradually, both men and women started crying, too, and breaking down with emotion. Shefali tried to control herself, but she wasn't successful. The priest knew that every funeral held emotional and tender moments. So, to lighten the moment, he told the guests they could symbolically throw the flowers and pious water after the funeral into the Delaware River.

The priest said, "Now, Shefali, you can ask forgiveness for any fault you have created in this lifetime."

In a low voice, Shefali asked, "Can I pray for relatives outside of my father's family? Can I say a prayer for someone whom I owe a lot of past favors?"

The priest told her she could and then asked who the gentleman was for whom she was praying. Shefali told him the relative was just like a father to her and that they had been very close.

"Your father's Gotra, I know. If you tell me the name and Gotra of this unknown person, his soul will be satisfied when the pious water is thrown into the platform."

"First, think about his face, take two fibrous twigs, and the pious water. Begin with a hymn, and then throw the pious water toward the sky."

Shefali started crying again even though she tried many times to control herself. It took several attempts to begin the hymn, but when she did, the words of the hymn were so touching that everyone in the room became mesmerized.

Subrata wondered to whom, outside of India and the Gotra, she was sending her prayer? Subrata did not understand; who was she was praying about?

She was only a few feet away from him, but he did not recognize who she was anymore. Thirty-two years of fog had surrounded her; the tears in her eyes were of sadness but also, there was some hot steam of repentance. As if Shefali was crying from a safe distance with her heart's invisible pretense.

"Oum! Kashyap Gotra, Grover Snyder deva sarmana… I am praying for my adopted father."

# 8

~~~~~~~~~

# The Ocean at Key West

*Chapter One*

I originally went to Key West on business; the design work for my engineering company was complete after only four days. This left three days to relax in the hotel garden, to walk the beach, and to explore the island by myself. Actually, the business meeting at Key West had just been an excuse to visit this beautiful part of Florida. I would use my time there to rest and unwind.

After the first day, I realized how popular and crowded the beach was – from early morning until the end of the day. There were throngs of people – families, couples, individual sun bathers - everywhere you looked; people were lying on blankets, jumping in the waves, and building sand castles.

Fighting through the crowds to get to the edge of the ocean was like finding your way through Bhul Bulaiya in Lucknow! However, by the end of the day, the crowds began to disappear, leaving only a few people behind.

As I felt the night breeze on my face, I thought about the next three days; I knew the night sky would produce an enormous, silvery full moon shining over us all. I imagined how the moon would look when it peeked over the branches of the palm trees or when it glittered on the water's surface. I expected nothing less than an enchanted, magical atmosphere.

Key West's beach began shortly after the main street ended and stretched as far as the eye could see. There was a row of bit-houses, standing systemically near a group of palm trees. A bigger building, with onion-colored paint, was the main restaurant, and I saw many hotels stretching into the distance. Every hotel seemed to have a small garden for guests to enjoy; that is where I was sitting when I saw an older man walking along the beach.

He had a walking stick in his right hand, and his suit was made of fine material. He didn't look toward the ocean as he walked, so I assumed he was not a newcomer to the ocean. He knew I was watching him, so he came straightaway toward me and asked, "Are you from India? Ah, wait...I assume you are Bengali."

I was surprised by his bold question because my clothing was very much American and besides, what would a Bengali be doing in Key West, Florida? How did he know?

Without an invitation, he sat next to me on the bench and said, "Your facial features seem to be Indian, but you are probably wondering how I knew that you are Bengali."

I shook my head and replied, "You are right...how did you know?"

"I knew you were not American; how many Americans would be sitting alone on the beach watching the waves? Americans are too busy with big, fancy cars and beautiful, young girls."

"You are not captivated by this ocean, too?" I asked.

"I come here frequently with Mandira, so the thrill of the ocean has become old to me."

"Who is Mandira?"

"Oh, yes! Mandira is my youngest brother's daughter; she is a sensitive and sweet young woman. You see, I live in Calcutta, my wife passed away two years ago, and I am a retired professor. Every year I visit America for several months."

"Is that the reason you are walking alone?"

"I am not alone. Mandira is here with me, but she has gone to buy some French fries. She will return shortly."

"That sounds nice – eating French fries and wandering the beach."

"Yes, her companionship is welcomed - I enjoy traveling, you see - and my niece is lovely company."

I realized that as a retired man, he was probably thoroughly bored living by himself. Traveling and seeing new places and meeting new people was probably the way he dealt with his boredom. Traveling with his niece must have been a pleasant distraction.

Mandira stepped onto the sand with French fries in her hand. She was a bit surprised to see her uncle talking to a stranger.

"Hello," she said, after eyeing me curiously.

Her uncle excitedly explained that I was a Bengali, and we had both been speaking the Bengali language until she entered the conversation.

"I have not told you my name," he exclaimed. "I am Amarish Shingha, and this is my niece, Mandira."

I told them my name, and looking at Mandira, I offered her my seat on the bench.

How odd that in Key West you would find a Bengali companion to spend time with! I glanced at the girl, from time to time, and guessed she was probably in her early twenties; she was indeed beautiful - with black intelligent eyes and a soft smile.

Mandira asked, "Uncle, do you want to walk closer to the water and see if we can find some shells?"

"Let this Florida beach go to hell. I prefer the beaches of Puri and the beach of Cox Bazaar in Bangladesh. The waves there are massive!"

Mandira shook her head and smiled.

Her uncle became excited talking about his native country. He said, "In Puri, they mix coconut water with Jermaine scotch whiskey...did you know that? On sunny days, you can see the beauty of Konarak and the capital city of Bhubaneswar; in the evening, you can sit on top of Jagannath in Puri and drink the whiskey drink. It is so much fun there!

"But here, in the morning, all you can hear is the ocean pounding on the shore and the noise of it at night."

Looking at Marinda, he said, "You will not understand the excitement that can be found in India; you only know what you think is excitement here in America."

Then, after seeing his niece's confused face, he added with a sly grin, "When is Sukumar coming to the beach? He was supposed to meet us here in Key West two days ago...and when he arrives, the real fun will start!"

I was floating on the speed of the gentleman's sentences, but I stopped at the mention of Sukumar. "Who is Sukumar?" I asked.

"Sukumar is a bright student working on his MBA in Jacksonville. He and Mandira became acquainted here in Key West last year. By the way, is that the reason we came here for vacation again this year?" her uncle looked at his niece and grinned.

Mandira looked down at the sand, shook her head, and pulled her uncle's arm to go walking.

## Chapter Two

The weather in Key West was constantly changing. In the early morning, the sweet sunshine rose above the slowly waking buildings of Main Street and peeked over the tops of the palm trees. The midday sun was hot and steamy and relentless, even though the beachgoers didn't seem to mind at all. By late afternoon, the sunset would melt like the yoke of an egg onto the surface of the water – soft colors of red and yellow and apricot.

As I watched the two of them walk to the water's edge, I realized that night was different than most. The sun had already sunk below the horizon, and the ocean water had begun to move to a silent rhythm. Soon, the waves erupted from the wind that whistled across its surface. From the hotel's garden, I sat and watched the changing weather; the wind began to swirl around my shoulders and to push Amarish and Marinda along the sand into the darkness.

As I was thinking about trying the whiskey drink Amarish had mentioned, I noticed a very handsome, young man sitting at the edge of the garden. I observed him quietly and noticed he was reading a National Geographic magazine that I had left on a table the previous night.

The man must have felt my gaze because he looked my way and said, "I assume this is your magazine? I hope you don't mind."

"Not at all," I answered. "Your accent tells me you are not from America. Are you Indian?"

"Yes, sir, I am."

"Which part of India do you call home?"

"Oh, I am from West Bengal."

I spread my arms wide into an open embrace and said with a smile, "What a surprise! I am also Bengali! Where do you live in America? How many days will you be staying in Key West?"

"I now live in Jacksonville, and I will be staying here until Monday. How long will your visit here be?"

"I'm afraid I will have to leave this paradise for New Jersey on Sunday morning. You see, I work there as an engineer, and my project here is complete. I came to America on an H-1 Visa, which will allow me to stay in this country as long as I want."

"It sounds like you are a lover of nature and of the ocean. Do you miss the weather along the Bay of Bengal?"

"Yes, I do miss my home country, but if I don't think of the weather or nature, then what will I think about?"

I continued, "How many places have you visited in America besides Key West?"

"I have not traveled to many places so far because I arrived a short time ago. Are there many places to roam in America?"

"Not really, most of the attractions are manmade – not cultural at all. Near the Colorado River in the Midwest there is a place called the Grand Canyon. It is thousands of miles long, and it reflects the land during prehistoric times. It is worth the trip!

"Then, in the east, there is Niagara Falls, and in the west, there is Yosemite National Park. All are breath-taking and incredibly beautiful. There doesn't seem to be much else to visit in America!" I laughed.

"So, if all of my meetings are held in the coastal towns of Florida, I am saved!"

"It sounds like you enjoy living near the ocean," replied the young man.

"Yes, I love being by the water - wherever I am. While in India, I used to travel to Puri at least two or three times a year. I also loved Chilka Lake and Gopalpur Beach. Plus, near our house, was my favorite – Digha - a beach resort on the Bay of Bengal.

"That is now in the past...there is no comparison to Puri."

"I also like the beaches of Puri; it is not as rough as the beach at Madras. I think that is why I love the weather in Key West; it reminds me of my home."

"Is it the weather here or the beauty of the ocean more to your liking?"

"Probably the beauty of the ocean is what attracts me more; the feeling one gets of the beach in the moonlight is unbelievable. However, I don't like the way the ocean changes when there is a full moon – the tides are high, the water has a life of its own, and the sounds of the crashing waves rattle through my brain. Sometimes, those sounds paralyze me."

While we were talking, old uncle and Mandira walked into the garden; I raised my hand and waved. A huge smile spread across

Amarish's face, and he began to laugh uncontrollably at the sight of Sukumar.

"So, here you are...finally! We have been waiting for you, Sukumar," Amarish said.

Mandira blushed.

"Let me stay here and talk with my new friend," he added, "while Mandira, you go walk with Sukumar. Tonight, there will be moonlight on the beach under a full moon – very romantic."

## Chapter Three

"Are you crying, Mandira?" Sukumar asked in a concerned voice.

"The grand beauty of the sea and the sky brings me to tears - tears of happiness. I am surrounded by stunning yet peaceful images! Do you feel the same?" she asked.

"Yes, the evening is breathtaking!" he said, as the two of them silently walked the water's edge.

"You know," he continued, after a few moments, "I feel we should talk of marriage. We have been apart for quite some time now – time enough to know our true feelings. As for me, I have the same feelings for you as I did when we first met."

Mandira began to giggle with joy but said nothing; her soft, poetic laugh rose in the air and settled on the ears of another couple. They were walking in the moonlight, too, and smiled as they passed – they understood.

"I must return to Jacksonville on Monday. When will I see you again? When can we discuss this matter?" he asked.

"Who knows when that will be? Oh...what makes life so difficult?"

"What makes our partnership so difficult? Are we afraid of our relative's thoughts or of society's reaction to our marriage? I have lived a good life and have owned a big house with expensive cars.

My bank account has always been overflowing, but none of these things have any meaning now. You are my jewel, the most valuable object in my life. I can't bear to leave without you."

Mandira replied, "I did not sleep well last night because I was afraid you would not come to me; I was afraid you were lost.

"And now, the sounds of the ocean are buzzing in my ears. Just the thought of you leaving makes me dizzy! The fishermen are catching fish in the darkness of the night; they do not fear the ocean. Then, why is my heart pounding so fiercely with every crashing wave?"

The air between them became silent. They moved closer to one another on the bench and interlocked arms. The love affair of a young couple that is based on friendship is enormously sweet. There is no binding responsibility yet, but it is so very romantic. Both parties knew that this episode had a final destination, and the emotions of that night would be like a rainbow in the sky – like a colored bubble, floating in their memories.

And the full moon smiled down upon them.

## Chapter Four

The next night, as I settled myself in the hotel's garden, Sukumar approached me and asked how I pass my time when visiting Key West. I started to explain my business connections and what I enjoyed during my free time.

Shortly, I noticed that he seemed to have left our conversation; he was staring blankly into space, and his eyes and face were a warm red color.

I wondered what could be wrong. Was the sound of the angry ocean connecting to Sukumar's mind and overcoming his own thoughts? Sukumar had told me of his fear of the ocean whenever the tides seemed to go mad.

I looked again, and his eyes had turned opaque; before I knew what had happened, he slid from his chair onto the floor and began moaning. I watched as his arms and legs started flailing around his body like the arms of a windmill.

At first, I thought he was having a heart attack, but I knew a seizure was not a symptom of a heart attack. Besides, he was of a young age, and most likely, this was not the reason for his seizure.

Without understanding, I ran to the hotel manager who promptly called for help. When the medics arrived, they held Sukumar's shoulders to the floor to calm the seizure, and they put a spoon in his mouth to prevent him from biting his tongue. They injected a medicine in his arm, and within minutes, Sukumar lay still.

The medics and I carried him to his room and laid him on his bed. I tucked him under the covers and watched his breathing while he slept. One medic explained that he had had an epileptic seizure, and he assured me he would eventually wake up with no recollection of what had happened.

I thought of calling Amarish to be by Sukamar's side, but I also wondered if this episode would pass unnoticed. Was it really something Mandira's uncle needed to know?

As I pondered these questions, I looked down at the beach. The tides were high and grabbing at the sand – in and out, in and out - the waves were roaring like a never-ending freight train. The whizzing noise of the evening was piercing my ears, so I closed the window and stepped back. I decided to keep silent and to go to my own room. I knew the waves would gradually subside; the full moon would be waning, and the beach would return to normal soon. I closed the door behind me.

The next day, I was surprised that Sukumar did not come to me to ask about the night before or to thank me for staying by his side. Possibly, he felt ashamed to talk of the incident, but we had been acquaintances for one day. Finally, I decided he must have forgotten everything – except Mandira – and had simply focused on other things.

I went about my day and, by evening, I found myself sitting next to Amarish, watching the beach from the garden. This time, both of us were gazing down on Sukumar and Mandira - two lovers on the beach.

They were sitting on the bench, side by side, as if the two friends were attached to one another - a couple with no division between them.

We both smiled.

I thought to myself how, in this world, God had created women like the coastline lying on the shore of an ocean. The waves come and go regularly, in a methodical pattern, and the rebel ocean floor is calmed by the engulfing flow of the water. God knew that if this were not so, men would remain an ocean without a sandy shore.

I turned to Amarish, "I will be leaving in the morning and returning to New Jersey. And you? How much longer will the two of you be here?"

He replied, "We are here for two more days, and Sukumar will return to Jacksonville on Monday."

I wondered if I should tell Amarish and Marinda about Sukumar's ailment. The four of us were merely road travelers. Should I let the friendship end on the road itself? Or does Marinda deserve to know Sukumar's entire story before beginning a new life as his wife? Maybe he has already confided in her; maybe they are already facing this challenge together. However, if I made the mistake of keeping his secret, the marriage might not begin on even ground. I knew I must explain to Mandira.

I looked down on the loving couple, and I could not move. The ocean looked so beautiful – indigo waves dancing with each other in a game of touch and go. Mile after mile, the beach was alive with small white fairy lights strung on every palm tree and every bench. The salty smell of the ocean settled in my nostrils. I couldn't disturb them now.

The two were wearing light jackets and holding hands, completely absorbed with one another.

"Do you know where your shortfall is?" Mandira asked.

"No, I do not know. Tell me."

"It is nowhere. You are perfect in every respect."

Listening to her cooing voice, Sukumar's face was dazzling in the sweet happiness of the moment; he squeezed Marinda's hand in his own.

Hearing such words, I wondered who I was to shatter a moment like this. The moment was rolling and smiling mischievously; the smaller waves loaded with stupid foolishness. It was as if the sea was telling me to linger a bit longer and to not snatch their happiness away so carelessly. It reminded me of the old cinema music:

"My dream girl lives inside,

The seven oceans and the thirteen river banks.

I sailed along the path,

And saw that radiant girl."

Sukumar and Mandira's dreamboats were sailing along with sheer happiness. The ocean had given them permission to sail before the full moon appeared again. Until then, the ocean would indulge them. Until then, neither society's interference nor my concerns would be boarding their dreamboat, unauthorized. Their marvelous gaiety was a moment's spark but not an eternal jingling sound.

# 9

*≺≺≺≺≺≺≺*

# A Mole

"You have just missed the train!" a voice uttered from the platform bench.

"Just my luck! The train was here a few seconds ago, and just before I reached the platform - it left! My day is ruined."

"You could try to catch the handle of the door; you might make it if you start running after the train now."

"Are you mad? Look at my hands! I have luggage in both hands, and I have a bundle under my arm as well. How could I possibly catch the train door's handle?

"I can't believe what has happened - look at how many bags of clothing my cousins have dumped on my body! It is as if they will never see me again," the traveler moaned.

"Let me tell you what I have done before while traveling. I place all the bundles in a big box and place them in the baggage car. If there is no space left in the box for the gifts, I simply keep the extra items in storage at the station. When next I come, I collect the packages and take them home with me at that time," the man on the bench smiled, as if solving a great dilemma.

"My God! How can you do that? If someone gives you gifts from their heart, how can you leave them in a solitary train station and refuse to take them with you?

"Besides, you have not met my elder aunt. She oversees every movement and every decision all family members make! She is always either crying loudly about something, or she is scolding someone for their actions."

"Oh, yes! I have definitely met someone like that before. Crying and giving everyone advice at the same time...."

"You have no idea what life is like when visiting my aunt!" the traveler continued. "When you visit a relative after being away for a long while, you would think they would change their mood and be happy that you are visiting – not complaining about every move."

"One would hope!" the stranger agreed. "Since I cannot say that I have witnessed your aunt's behavior first-hand, I will have to imagine her judgmental, reprimanding stares. As of late, my imagination has become my constant companion, and it has proven to be extremely useful."

The stranger laughed, "How far do you think your imagination can take you?"

"The perspective of my imagination is all-encompassing, you know. Whatever I do not see with my own two eyes will always be reflected clearly in my mind - and just like that, the seedlings of my thoughts are spread!

"As a matter of fact, I can't go a day without using my imagination. For instance, if I visualize other peoples' movements in my mind, I can hold tightly to the images and reflect on those people and places for a long time.

"You see, I don't invite visitors into my home very often," the stranger continued, "because it creates a lot of difficulties for my family and me; however, if I focus on a stranger's life and on their experiences, interesting information will pop into my imagination in no time. Colors, smells, textures – my mind embraces all these things when I use my imagination.

"For example, have you noticed that every home has a different smell when you first enter? There are smells in my home which are totally different than the smells in your home. Most people do not understand this because, in their house, their continuous breathing camouflages the peculiar smell. Which smell is more pleasing? There is no difference; each is determined by the person's up-bringing and their life experiences. That is how to really appreciate their thoughts and actions. Do you understand what I am saying?"

"It sounds like you spend a good amount of time in your imaginary world. Does living in your imagination bring you temporary happiness? Is this how you envision every aspect of your life?" asked the traveler.

"Why, yes, I live happily in my imagination. Most days, it is the safest place to reside," replied the stranger.

"Look, do you have a regular doctor in this area whom you visit occasionally? Can you recall the atmosphere of the waiting room?"

"Yes, with my children. I have had to run to a local doctor's office several times," the traveler said. "Most of the time for a cold or a sore throat, minor cuts and fractures on the hands and legs, little bits of difficulties from time to time."

"Now, stop and visualize the waiting room - the surroundings covered with that peculiar smell, nurses running helter-skelter, and sick patients looking hopelessly at the receptionist. Why, even the chairs look pale and restless! Can you see this?"

With a blank stare, the traveler said, "No, I do not see them clearly...why? I do not understand."

The stranger ignored the question and continued, "The chair in the doctor's office where you sat one day will be occupied by someone else the next day. Like you, the next patient will be worrying unnecessarily about whether or not he is suffering from some rare, unknown disease. And there will be a different patient sitting there the next day and the next and the next.

"Does this vision fill you with ideas of how different sick patients think and worry about different things – all sitting in the same chair but with different concerns?" questioned the stranger.

"To hell with your outrageous imagination! I do not think such things because, if I did, I would break down from the stress and concern for those sad individuals!" chided the traveler, stepping closer to the man on the bench.

"That is the exact opposite of how you should react. You should not own other people's difficulties and drown yourself in their sadness. Instead, you should try to empathize with their situation and their sadness; then, you would not be pulled down by their misery, and you would be a lot better off. Now, do you understand?"

"No, I still do not understand. Are you saying that I am not capable of feeling the emotions of other humans? That I dismiss their emotions and their love-hate relationships in favor of my own thoughts?" the traveler asked.

"I did not say that at all, but if you feel the sorrow of other people – really sense the emotions they are experiencing - do you also understand and empathize with their pathos?"

"No, the world does not work that way! That is absurd! Are you telling me when you experience this emotional insight into other people's feelings, the situation creates an uncontrollable feeling in your heart? An aching? All because you used your imagination?"

"Exactly!" exclaimed the stranger. "I always try to catch the other fellow's feelings in my imagination; in my mind, I try to resurrect some kind of understanding and feeling of my own."

The traveler stopped and said, "For the sake of this discussion, let's imagine our places were reversed, and I am the person sitting on your bench. Let's imagine that YOU have missed the train and YOUR family is worried. I am trying to imagine what I would have done in that kind of situation."

"If I were sitting alone," the traveler continued, "I would be thoroughly bored, and what does a common man do when he is bored? Must he have many random thoughts to pass the time?"

The stranger's eyes widened, "Precisely the question...other than being bored sitting on a bench, you have no complaints – you are either happy or restless. In order to increase your happiness, you scratch your memory to evoke emotions from your imagination. Today tears on your cheeks may seem salty, but tomorrow, those same tears might become a scent of a memory. Perhaps today's misery will become tomorrow's victory."

The stranger continued excitedly, "Another example, my friend...have you noticed the room next to the station master's quarters? There is a woman lurking there. Do you see her?"

The traveler squinted in the general direction. "No, I see no one," he replied.

"Oh, yes...there is lady there; she is my wife."

"Your wife? This is an unusual time for your wife to be in this empty railway station. Where is she? I don't see her."

"She is there, hiding from me and on constant watch. She thinks I do not see her; sometimes I want to call her name and tell her to go home, but if I scold her, she will only go back into hiding.
"

"Look at her...she never eats properly or gets enough sleep. Her hair is a mess, her skirt is dirty and torn, and she is not even forty years old! She is like a broken doll on a shelf, and no one wants to play with her. I can see she is suffering for my sake and my sake only. She is so very stubborn! Look at her peering around the door at me!"

"She never speaks to me when she is hiding; she will only cry relentlessly," the stranger scoffed indignantly.

"Whenever I go out, she finds me and begs me to stay home with her like a pet dog on her lap. She won't allow me to smoke anymore, and she wishes I would remain in bed from morning 'til night. She wants to fawn over me – to sing to me in a low voice, to stroke my brow."

"Look at her again, looking at me from her hiding place. Do you see her?" the stranger queried.

"No, I do not see her. There is no one there. You are insane!"

"I am not insane; I am only using my imagination and seeing my wife as I know she is," the stranger replied, with a knowing smile.

"Maybe she is worried about you – about your health, about being in these crowds, about being lost in the city."

The stranger ignored his suggestions. "And what about the station master? I see him there, day after day in his office; if you listen to his thoughts, he is thinking about what he will do after his shift or about what he will do tomorrow on his day off. He might also die tonight! No one knows for sure," the stranger argued, as he looked deep into the traveler's eyes. "People are always different if you take the time to learn their background."

The traveler shuddered and began to turn from the stranger, searching uncomfortably for the next train.

"Wait...please don't leave. Will you please come toward me; I want to show you something very peculiar. Near my neck, just under my beard, can you see some cut marks?" he asked, while pulling his beard aside so the traveler had a clear view. "Next to the cut mark, there is a mole the size of a raisin. My doctor has determined this small mole is a cancerous spot – malignant cancer. That word, malignant, is quite a fruitful word, don't you think? Malignant...malignant. That spot is a spot of death. Whenever and however death arrives, we must be prepared beforehand."

"I am trying hard to hide this mole with the thickness of my beard. Who knows...the hand of Yamaduta may go down the wrong road by mistake if he cannot find me. How can I quietly play this treacherous game with the Death God, Yama, if I am not prepared? The mole can be very painful from time to time, but the game is a game all the time. What do you think?"

"Sadly, you are right! I am sorry you are suffering from cancer."

"Everybody suffers from cancer; some have it on their brain, some on other parts of their body. Half of summer is gone, but I have not fully tasted the mango fruit yet. Neither have I tasted the litchi fruit of Majaffarpur. Have you noticed the litchi fruit is like a woman's sweet lips? How sweet and moist they are!"

"Have you checked your watch for the time of the next train?" the stranger asked abruptly.

"Yes, I have, but there is no time left for me; there are no more trains for the evening," the traveler moaned. "My life is in a turmoil."

"No, my friend. You are the one who has plenty of time left."

"Would you please do me a favor before the next train?" the stranger asked. "I see in my imagination you live in the township, and you have planted a few flowers in your garden."

"I know the bellflowers are in blossom now, and I hope you can make at least one garland of these delicate flowers," he continued. "Will you please count the number of bellflower buds on the garland as you work?"

"Please...see how many buds you count as you create. You see, the number of blossoms you count will also be the number of months I have to live the rest of my life," the stranger implored.

"Please calculate the number of flowers slowly. Be sure you are precise. I do not want my wife to be distraught by your results – she can be such a sweet, delicate thing. Please count slowly, very slowly."

# 10

❧❧❧❧❧❧❧❧

# A Marriage –
# Yankee & Bengali Style

*Chapter One*

The place was Westchester County, New York. The occasion was the annual Bengali conference in America. The conference center was packed with approximately six thousand Bengalis. Every room had an invisible crowd. Typical American clothing styles were mixed with cultural Bengali dress - dhotis and long-sleeve punjabis. Everywhere the Bengali language was mixed with American slang. A new language - Yankeli - actually sounded good to the ears!

In the heart, there seemed to be an emotional flow of past Bengali culture; in the air, there was a Bengali style, and in the sky, there was a never-aging Bengali sentiment.

On this happy occasion, after a gap of twenty-five years, there was an ignorant mixing of two old students from Calcutta College – Mr. Sanatan Bhattacharya and Mr. Sam Bonnergy. In their previous culture, Mr. Sanatan had been a petty Brahmin of Howrah District, and Mr. Bonnergy had been half-Bengali from Poss Alipur of Calcutta.

They were never close friends, but meeting after twenty-five years, their minds became soaked with emotion. They wished each other's family a warm greeting, and their wives, Bela and Lindi, with folded hands, welcomed each other graciously.

The children also acknowledged one another; Sanatan's son, Ananda (or Andy), and Sam's daughter, Sujata (or Sue), bowed pleasantly.

Sanatan had come to the conference in order to maintain his status in the Hindu cultural field, his wife had come to look at the sari selection, and Andy joined the conference to conduct a meeting representing his younger generation.

Sam had come to the conference to watch his daughter dance, and his wife had come to the conference to find a marriage partner for their daughter.

Andy was an excellent choice as speaker for the second-generation conference; his speech was excellent and to the point while his manner of addressing the audience was gracious yet confident.

Lindi was an American beauty – soft, white skin that made her look like a China doll - who had married Sam in spite of her parent's protests. She was a college professor, was amazing at running the Bonnergy household, and was a wonderful cook of all manner of Indian dishes...and she was very moved by Andy's presence. She complimented Sanatan and Bela several times regarding their son's performance.

Toward the end of the conference, Sujata danced a classic Indian dance, Bharat Natyam, which was superb! It was an excellent performance with the music and rhythm enhancing her every move. The audience was speechless...and so were Sanatan and Bela.

They were both thrilled by her performance, and they clapped loudly and vigorously when the dance ended. They both thought she looked elegant in her beaded dress and her fine jewelry.

Sanatan complimented Sam several times and compared Sujata's movements to an angel with wings.

"Our son should find this very type of girl and make her his bride," he said.

Bela replied, "You should stop saying such things. Every time you see a beautiful, young girl, you think of her as your son's prospective wife. Andy is not that old – he is only twenty-eight years!"

"Twenty-eight is not a young man. He is old enough to be married and to raise a family."

"You want your son to get married at twenty-eight – so very young - just like you did?" she asked.

"Yes, I would love to see him get married," Santana argued. "He has enjoyed himself as a single man for the past several years. It is time he found a beautiful wife with whom he can settle down and raise a family.

"Being married at an early age is not entirely satisfying. We got married when I was the age of eighteen; can't you see that even before I turned fifty years old, everything in our life was old and settled? If our son were to marry, he would avoid that feeling; he would have the best of both worlds."

"That is advice you read in a book! In America, the more time spent as a single person before getting married means that single person will be more undisciplined later in life."

"That is entirely wrong," Sanatan maintained. "When a man is married, he will sit and eat like a hungry animal."

He looked at her silently and shook his head, as if he had no hope of changing her mind. Quickly, he changed the subject, "What do you think of my friend, Bonnergy?"

Bela replied, "Do you mean the short, ugly old man? He talked forever and went on and on about nothing in particular!"

"But how about his wife, Lindi? Did you like her?"

"Fat old woman..."

"Well then, how did you like their daughter, Sujata?"

"She has a likable figure, and her face is okay. After wearing expensive jewelry, she looked much better."

"How many girls in this country have a beautiful face like you, Bela? If your son's new wife is more beautiful than you, can you tolerate that?" he grinned.

"No one can out-shine me, even if I am an older woman. In my youth, I was more beautiful and elegant than most. When I painted my mouth with turmeric paste, my face would glow like the full moon," she smiled, remembering.

In a hotel a block away, there was a similar conversation between Lindi and Sam Bonnergy. Lindi asked Sam, "Are you enjoying time with your old friend?"

"He is the same dull-witted and stupid person I remember from Calcutta. Plus, he hiccups loudly around other people. I had forgotten he possessed that habit."

"Well, what about your friend's wife? What did you think of her?"

Sam scoffed, "She is a first-class, spoiled child; nothing seemed to please her. Her eyes look like a dinosaur!"

"And what about Andy? You have not mentioned him."

"Well, he appeared intelligent and looked quite masculine. He seemed nice enough."

Lindi smiled and her nostrils flared, "What about a marriage proposal between Sujata and Andy? What do you think about that idea?"

Sam looked at her in surprise. "Are you mad?" he said. "The Bhattacharya family is very uncultured with no sophistication whatsoever. I am not sending a marriage proposal to that idiotic, uneducated family!"

"A marriage is not arranged by Sanatan Bhattacharya himself, but by his son, too. Did you notice how refined and well-mannered

Andy appeared? He is also pursuing an outstanding business career – which would be an asset."

"Where did you learn so much about Andy? And what about Sujata? Will she even like Andy?"

"Remember that I am a professor with an MBA; I know many things about this life. Who runs the family budget, and who controls the decisions?" she asked.

"Of course, I will discuss Andy with Sujata first," his wife continued. "If she says no to our suggestion, then I will not proceed further. Don't forget - if we set the bar high, then Sujata will end up living a high life, also."

Sam thought for a minute and then smiled, "You know, I like the way you think! This might work out after all, my darling!"

Lindi did not stop there; she found even more information about Sanatan's family. She found out Andy and his father had more money and more influence than previously thought. As far as Sanatan's ugly cultural background, that was something that could be overlooked. After all, her family had not been so accepting of Sam's cultural background when they met initially, and they had married anyway and had enjoyed a long and solid marriage; she had no regrets.

Sujata agreed with her mother – Andy would make a wonderful husband. So, that was that; Lindi decided that Andy would be Sujata's prospective bridegroom.

At first, when Sanatan learned of the marriage proposal, he was shocked by Sam and Lindi's idea. Then, he allowed himself to really think through her suggestion. He liked the idea of having a connection with the respectable Bonnergy family from Calcutta. He had achieved a fairly high status in the American business world; the only thing he lacked was cultural status, and this would solve the problem.

After all, the girl was nice looking, and she might not fight and argue with his wife since she came from a well-mannered, cultured family. Besides, her skin was quite pale so their grandchildren would be of a lighter color, which would be different than his family.

However, Bela was not that pleased upon hearing of the marriage proposal. She was very old-fashioned in her thinking. How many prospective brides' parents would beg her for Andy's hand in marriage? She wasn't sure he should say "yes" to this marriage; maybe he should wait to see what other proposals came his way.

A mother's eyes cannot be easily deceived, and Bela had to admit that she had noticed Andy's actions; even in the short time he was in NYC, he had spoken several times with Sujata. Did he like Sujata, too?

However, Bela did not agree to this proposal immediately. "My daughter-in-law should come to the marriage with jewelry that covers her entire body; otherwise, there will be no marriage," she insisted.

"The days of the bride bringing a dowry to a marriage are over," Sanatan replied.

"No! The day of a bride's dowry are not over; instead of being referred to as a dowry, people nowadays call them wedding gifts.

"We have spent thousands of dollars on our son's education. Do you not want to recover some of our expenses?"

"Yes but do American-raised girls even wear gold jewelry as ornaments anymore?" he wondered aloud.

"They might not be interested now, at a younger age, but when they grow older, their ambition of nobler objects will increase. The younger girls do not wear gold jewelry around the house or to their workplace, but they wear them to social functions, weddings, and other events.

"They have a ruby set, an emerald set, a pearl set, and even a diamond set.

"How much purchasing power does Sujata have, do you know?" she asked.

Sanatan had noticed that when Bela spoke of such things – diamonds, rubies, and emeralds – her lips curled up, and she had a reddish glow about her face. She started to look glassy-eyed and excited.

"Once you begin talking about the gold and diamonds, you do not want to stop, do you?" he mused.

"No, I do not, and I do not want to change this conversation! You are a dull engineer! What do you know about valuable jewelry and exquisite sari? All you ever see around you are those beautiful motor cars and young, female bodies!"

Sanatan was furious. "Oh, how many times do you crow like a sly fox? I have no choice but to look at beautiful white girls. Have you seen our friend, Robert's, wife? She does not wear gold jewelry, but she is so elegant and beautiful. Her body is soft and smooth like a pigeon!"

Bela didn't let up – she continued her tirade. "What did you say? Did you compare my body to an old crow? Not soft like a pigeon?

"After a day's work, I come home and cook Indian dishes for you, clean the house, wash all the clothes; how can I keep my hands and my skin soft like my younger days? Be careful, your words are gradually going down twisted roads!"

Sanatan gently caught hold of Bela's hand and said, "We are talking about our son's marriage and that pleasant talk has led to a fight between us...that is not a good thing."

Bela agreed and smiled shyly, wrapping her arms around her husband.

Sanatan had to eventually admit his defeat when it came to Bela's jewelry proposal; he knew she would not budge an inch on the subject. So, he negotiated with Sujata's family that her body be covered in jewels on the day of the wedding.

At the same time, he did not back down from his own requirements. Sanatan insisted the marriage take place in Calcutta and that it followed the Indian tradition of body spraying with turmeric. All the hymns were to be sung in classic Sanskrit; no hymns would be translated into English.

Lindi had learned from her own life that in a typical Bengali-style marriage, the dowry was the most important part. After the marriage, the wife would live a peaceful life depending on how much give and take occurred during the union, and everyone knew a wife's giving had to be a minimum of ninety percent.

After getting their list from Sanatan, Lindi was not disturbed at all. There were many times she had dealt with colleagues during meetings at her college for matters of money, so she knew the exchange rate was one dollar per seventy-five rupees.

Sujata would be all right; Lindi would propose that whatever she had in gold bonds, she would give half to Andy. He could change the solid gold whenever he wanted, but there was no reason to cash them in now because the road is full of thieves.

After the final meeting between the two families, Lindi took a beautiful gold bracelet from her bag and tucked it into Bela's hand and said, "Whether the marriage takes place or not, this bracelet is yours."

Bela's heart melted like ice cream.

It was decided the marriage would take place in Calcutta. Neither the bride nor the groom had more than seven days leave, so the honeymoon would be celebrated in America after the marriage had been performed successfully.

## Chapter Two

Sanatan was an engineer, so it was no surprise that he planned the wedding in great detail. Many relatives came to the ceremony, and both families flew to Calcutta two days before the festivities.

Both families paid special attention to the gifts of American money that started pouring into the bridegroom and his bride like a stream of unending water. An old proverb says: "If money is spent plenty, then even the tiger's milk is available." Both families saw this adage coming true right before their eyes.

Everyone suffered jet lag from their trip and were very drowsy the first day; however, by the wedding day, all tired eyes followed every little detail of the Indian marriage.

It began with the groom wearing an Indian dhoti on top of his American pants, and the bride wearing her exquisite sari dress, which made her look like a vision from another world. Everyone present could see the happiness in their eyes, as if they couldn't contain their excitement of the day.

The only problem that arose during the ceremony was with the prayer hymns that were originally written in Sanskrit. Not all guests knew what was being said, so the ritual came to a stand-still while everything was translated to proper English.

In spite of this interruption, Sanatan was happy that, according to the classical acts, things were moving forward. In any case, the marriage proceeded systematically with no more problems.

After the dinner, Andy and Sujata mingled with their guests and shared their excitement with everyone, while giving their thanks for the major part they had played in their glorious day.

## Chapter Three

When the marriage celebration came to an end, the couple planned to return to New York City where they would resume their work with the idea of taking a honeymoon in six months' time – after acquiring more leave from their jobs.

But the water of Calcutta is different than anywhere in the world; even God does not know what will happen tomorrow in the city.

Three separate events occurred that changed the couple's plans.

The first incident began with the bridegroom's parents; Sanatan and Bela liked to eat fresh prawn and lobster – very much! On the night of the marriage, they both ate a large number of lobsters – twenty-two lobsters to be precise. They must have eaten some fiber scales as well. That night, there was very little sleep in their bedroom.

In addition, they drank much water without boiling it first. These actions all came to a head the following morning. They were supposed to leave Calcutta, but they kept running to the bathroom – again and again – and being sick to their stomach. Trying to ease their pain, they both lay on the beds in their room like two cut banana trees until help arrived.

Diarrhea is a common ailment in Calcutta, so two doctors were called to the house, one quite old and the other quite young. They could not be sure what had caused the attack, but they assumed it started with the water the two had drank. Water in Calcutta needs to be boiled at least two times before drinking it; unfortunately, Sanatan and Bela had not taken this precaution.

The second incident happened when Lindi emerged from the Kalighat Temple of Goddess Kali. She had studied the Bengali style of celebrating a wedding because she wanted everything to be perfect for her daughter and to be in the Bengali way. So, she watched the Goddess in the temple, and she purchased a lot of red-flowered garlands for Sujata.

Lindi also demanded to travel to the wedding site by rickshaw, to observe the Calcutta life-style firsthand, instead of taking a taxi. As they rode, she tentatively watched the sights and sounds of the Calcutta streets; while she was looking on with curiosity, Bonnergy was looking at the thin and beautiful girls walking by.

The rickshaw moved slowly because of the extra weight of the two passengers, when it abruptly hit a pothole in the street. The rickshaw couldn't keep its balance, and it fell sideways with a loud crash. Even though they were holding on tightly, Lindi and Sam were thrown from the carriage. Lindi, with her hoarse-sounding screams, landed in the street on one side of the rickshaw, while Sam's massive body landed squarely on the street on the other side of the rickshaw.

The sight of a white-skinned woman with a red-flower garland in her hair and wearing a colored sari surprised everyone in the street. When the excitement died down, several pedestrians rushed to help Lindi, and they carried her to the nearest doctor. The doctor was not there, but the compounder, his assistant, took a look at her to see if he could help. He carefully looked at her leg, which appeared to be swollen.

"Your leg is severely damaged. Soon, the swelling will be worse and will change in three stages," he explained. "First, it will swell like a potato, and then it will swell even more, like luchi or fried bread. Finally, your leg will become enlarged like a drum.

"You should not walk on this leg at all, and you should have an x-ray performed as soon as possible."

In the meantime, Sam was sitting idly on the street; no one paid much attention to the old, fat Bengali. His left eye was swollen like a pumpkin, and his face was covered with black marks from hitting the sidewalk face first. As he sat and tried to get his wits about him, a loitering pavement bull came up to him and started licking his cheek with his long tongue. Bonnergy silently cursed the silly bull and hoped it would go away soon!

The third incident happened quietly among the bride and groom's relatives; they all decided the honeymoon should happen in India, not America, and both the bride and groom should send messages to their employers telling them they were staying in India for a while.

The relatives sent messages (in the young couple's names) and told their employers that a sudden labor strike had paralyzed Calcutta. All the transportation had stalled, and even life seemed to be postponed. They told them they would both return on a flight the next week.

Then, the relatives bought train tickets to Puri Konarak, the exotic city in the eastern part of India. Arrangements were also made for the hotel in Konarak. When the bride and groom heard this news, they immediately changed their plans and started for Konarak City.

During the marriage ceremony, both the bride and the groom had difficulty speaking the classic marriage hymns in Sanskrit, and they didn't understand what all the fuss had been about. Now that they were on the train, they talked and laughed in American slang as if they were the only people on the train.

The other first-class passengers did not understand the mixing of this English–Bengali language. The youngsters looked like Bengalis, but their accent was very confusing. To look at Andy's skin color and the way he was dressed, he appeared to be Anglo-Indian. And Sujata looked like a perfect Bengali bride with her white-colored skin and her face covered with red-colored vermillion. They both seemed quite happy and talked incessantly with one another.

Who would ask them whether their marriage was half-Bengali and half-American style...or maybe a full Yankeli (Yankee and Bengali) style?

# The Total Life Story of Dilip Kr Mukherjee:

- Multi-talented engineer; published author in literature and engineering.
- Graduated in engineering in 1961 with Second Rank
- Immigrated to America in 1979
- Wrote several steel specifications books with selected Indian Committee
- Obtained prestigious prize money from Steel Founders Society of America – 1995
- Included in 'Who's Who in Science and Engineering'
- Wrote fourteen books in Indian language beginning in 1992. Praised highly by famous Satyen Bose, Subhas Mukherji, and Nirendra Neth Chakraverty of India.
- Complimented highly by Mr. Shyamal Ganguli, Md. Siraj, Jay Goswami, Suchitra Mitra, Dinendra Chowdhury, and many prominent authors and celebrities of Calcutta, London, Australia, and New York
- In 1996, he was awarded and honored by C.A.B. of North America
- Voice of America took his interview in 1997
- In 1997, he was awarded Jajan Puroscar in Bengal academia and Indian Durdarshan published its nightly broadcast
- In 2019, he published his first English book of poetry, The Restricted Heaven, through Amazon and was highly appreciated by many American citizens, which is still continuing